PRACTICING THE PIANO

HOW STUDENTS, PARENTS, AND TEACHERS CAN MAKE PRACTICING MORE EFFECTIVE

By Nancy O'Neill Breth

ISBN 978-1-4234-8942-9

HAL•LEONARD® CORPORATION

7777 W. BLUEMOUND RD. P.O. BOX 13819 MILWAUKEE, WI 53213

In Australia Contact:
Hal Leonard Australia Pty. Ltd.
4 Lentara Court
Cheltenham, Victoria, 3192 Australia
Email: ausadmin@halleonard.com.au

Visit Hal Leonard Online at
www.halleonard.com

*To the memory of my mother, who frequently
told me that she loved listening to my practicing.*

TABLE OF CONTENTS

ACKNOWLEDGMENTS

It would be impossible to acknowledge every person who has contributed ideas for this book, since the list would include scores of teachers, students, friends, and family members from whom I have learned not just how to practice, but how to love doing it. The concepts at the heart of the practice tips in this book have come down through generations of teachers and students and continue to be passed around from musician to musician.

I am especially indebted to the late Margaret Saunders Ott, my high school piano teacher. She opened a new world to me many years ago and continued to encourage and inspire me for the next 50 years. Mrs. Ott never ran out of practice ideas and never got over the thrill of making music.

I thank Richard Smith, Victoria Wyatt, and Douglas Harrington for reading early versions of the manuscript and offering suggestions that significantly improved it. All errors and other lapses are, of course, entirely mine.

The greatest help of all came from my husband, Steven. If this book succeeds, it's because of him.

Nancy O'Neill Breth
Washington D.C.

INTRODUCTION

Practicing a musical instrument can be interesting, rewarding, even exciting. It can also be boring, maddening, and a dreaded responsibility. But one thing about practicing never changes: anyone who hopes to master a musical instrument has to do it.

I know well the frustration of a poor practice session, but most of the thousands of hours I've spent practicing over the years have brought me great satisfaction. A beautiful piece of music is awe-inspiring in itself. Puzzling out how to overcome its challenges—in other words, how to practice—is intriguing. And being able to play a piece well in the end is a joy.

What many music students struggle with is the act of practicing. They don't know how to use their time in a way that makes practicing both satisfying and effective. Consequently, one of the most common questions teachers hear is, how should I practice?

The purpose of this book is to answer that question by offering a broad selection of practice tips that do solve pianistic problems, but that also make practicing something to look forward to and enjoy.

Practicing the Piano is intended for music lovers of every age and stage. It explains in a nutshell why and how to examine a piece of music before starting to practice it, how to begin a new piece without planting bad habits, and how to organize practice time. It lays out how best to practice a piece from early stages through finishing touches. It suggests ways to get comfortable at the keyboard and stay that way, to develop speed without sacrificing accuracy, and to make music expressive. It gives advice on memorizing, preparing for performance, and bringing an old piece back to life.

The core of the book consists of over 150 specific tips that will enliven anyone's practice sessions. There are separate chapters addressed to parents of young students and to teachers, and there is a chapter on the interaction between student, teacher, and parent.

Although in my teaching I seldom make a strict separation between musical and mechanical practicing, this book does deal more with the mechanical side of piano playing. I hope that by offering assistance in the physical training of pianists this book will give students and their teachers more time and freedom to explore the soul of the music.

The practice tips in this guide come not only from my own experience but from my teachers, the community of teachers around me, and even from my students. Techniques of effective practicing have been handed down and passed around by generations of teachers of piano and other instruments. They are not tied to any one style or philosophy of teaching or performing. They work for various ages and levels of advancement because the vocabulary is straightforward, but the concepts are sophisticated enough to challenge even advanced pianists.

The better you play an instrument, the more fun it is to practice. Professional musicians typically love practicing and wish they had more time for it. Adult amateurs may even regard practicing as a kind of refuge from everyday life, even though they have to struggle to fit it into that life.

But for beginners of all ages, especially for precollege students, practicing can be a hard road. School and homework gobble up a huge part of the day, so fitting in daily practice is a constant challenge.

On the other hand, the very fact of music's complexity is one reason that people love it. It's not simple, it's not easy, but it is beautiful and intriguing. And unraveling complicated problems can be enormously gratifying, as any puzzle enthusiast can tell you. Also, the act of playing an instrument, especially the piano, can bring instant sensory pleasure: it feels good under the fingers and sounds wonderful to the ears.

Such rewards come just as much to beginners as to advanced players. Music draws us to itself and, on a good day, satisfies us like few other things in our lives. The very act of practicing—even long before a piece has been mastered—can bring deep satisfaction. That's what this book offers: interesting, adventuresome techniques to make your practicing so effective that it's fun, yes fun, to do.

THE PRACTICE PACT

The first step on the road to enjoyable and productive practicing is to make a pact with yourself—a pact to practice with *patience*, *attention*, *curiosity*, and *tunnel vision*.

Patience

Think of practicing as a part of your daily routine, like brushing teeth, getting dressed, working, going to school, or eating dinner. Nothing that must be done every day is fascinating every time. Set out with the understanding that practicing will be everything from exhilarating to agonizing. Take delight in the good days, and be patient when the going gets rough. All your work will pay off.

Attention

Make your practice time count. Keep the room quiet. Ask family members to stay in other parts of the house or at least to move quietly. Turn on the answering machine and turn off the computer, TV, and other electronic attention grabbers. Put a notepad on the piano so that if a nonmusical idea pesters you, you can write it down and then return to your music.

When you practice, devote 100 percent of your attention to the task. Listen as though your hands belonged to someone else, so that you hear exactly how you really sound.

Curiosity

Get in the habit of quizzing yourself. When a problem arises, start asking questions immediately. Ask yourself, for example,

> *What* happened? *Why*? *How* can I fix it?
>
> How did that sound? Was it better than before? If so, how? If not, why not?
>
> Should I slow down?
>
> What would the composer want this to sound like?
>
> Why is this *crescendo* here?
>
> How loud should this accent be?

Tunnel Vision

Take small steps in each practice session. Set specific, realistic goals. Focus on one problem at a time and apply practice drills to one short section at a time. Even within a section, work on one hand (or one musical line) at a time. Or you can concentrate on a single aspect, such as accuracy, rhythm, balance, dynamics, or tone quality.

PRACTICE TOOLS

Each time you are about to begin a practice session, make sure that several tools are within reach:

A *marker*—pencil, highlighter, stickers, or removable highlighter tape. Think of the musical score as your workbook. Feel free to write in visual aids like fingering, accidentals, pedal marks, dynamics, notes of encouragement, or danger signals.

A *music dictionary*. Musical terms are a composer's way of explaining how a piece should be played. Traditionally, these words are in Italian—*moderato*, for example, or *forte*. You want to understand every message the composer sends you, so you need a dictionary of musical terms to make that possible.

A *metronome*. This device can help you to track the beat, unravel complicated rhythms, raise a piece's tempo in tiny increments, feel a phrase, or just calm yourself down. Your teacher will guide you in the use of a metronome, but you can also find many uses for it on your own. And remember to stay alert when using the metronome. Some people turn it on but turn off their ears. It won't help you unless you actually hear it.

A good recorder. No one can remember all the details of a lesson. A recording greatly increases the value of each lesson by preserving everything that happened and allowing you to review the details during your practice sessions. Video helps even more than audio, since it allows you to see as well as hear your teacher's demonstrations. Listen to the recording the day after your lesson. Refer to it during the week whenever you need clarification or inspiration.

Later, especially when a piece is nearly ready to perform, record yourself and listen to the replay. The recording will tell you how you actually sound. If you're not happy with the results, you may learn from the recording what is missing.

A practice journal. It can be highly motivating to note milestones in your practice progress. Use a small notebook to keep track of practice sessions, jotting down specific goals, time spent, problems solved, pieces learned.

WHAT PRACTICING IS, AND ISN'T

A person can practice effectively in a hundred different ways. Good practicing never stays the same. It changes from hour to hour, from day to day, from year to year. That's because our moods vary, our capacity grows, the music itself changes, and our perspective on the music evolves.

For all of the aesthetic and emotional properties of music, playing an instrument is still a physical skill. Like learning to swim or play tennis or soccer, learning the piano is a process of physical training. To progress beyond the beginning stage, the pianist must build technique and endurance, and this requires massive amounts of repetition over time.

For far too many piano students, practicing means sitting down at the piano, opening the music to the first page, and playing the piece through. When their fingers trip, it's back to the beginning, and start again. And again, and again. That isn't practicing. Yes, it is possible to learn a piece by rote. But playing by rote opens the door to a slew of accidental errors, errors that become etched into the brain and later take enormous time and energy to correct.

When a student brings learned mistakes to a lesson, the lesson becomes little more than a correction session, disheartening for both student and teacher. Although everyone enjoys playing through pieces, if your ultimate goal is to learn a piece well and perhaps even to memorize and perform it, put away the casual play-throughs and start true practicing.

Because every new piece contains technical challenges, the question is always, how can I make the hard parts easy? The answer is, repetitive drills. You drill until you can play a challenging passage almost without thinking.

Repetition can be interesting and even fun if you use concise drills that engage the mind and imagination while training the body. Initially, drills will take more time than merely playing through a piece over and over. But once the drills become a part of your routine, your practicing will be more gratifying and you'll get better results. When physical movements become automatic, playing the piece is vastly more enjoyable. Then you can begin to focus on deeper issues, like what the music means to you and how you can convey this to others.

BUDGETING YOUR TIME

Learning to play the piano cannot be done in a hurry. It takes time—day by day, week by week, and over the years. Yet everyone is short of time. Children have school, homework, and sports; adults have jobs and family responsibilities. Time is precious because there never seems to be enough of it. So if you want to excel, finding the time to practice must become a priority.

Start by determining what time you have available, aside from job or school, and how you use that time. Make a chart of one week in your life. Decide what portion of each day you can devote to practicing, and make sure it is a time and an amount that you can do faithfully. Morning is the most productive time for many people. It's a good idea, especially for young students, to divide daily practice into two or three segments.

Write your practice time choices into your week's schedule along with all your other activities. If you are in school it might look like this:

	Mon	Tues	Wed	Thurs	Fri	Sat	Sun
6:30	Bkfast	Bkfast	Bkfast	z–z–z–	Bkfast	z–z–z–	z–z–z–
7:00	**practice**	**practice**	**practice**	Bkfast	**practice**	z–z–z–	z–z–z–
7:30	school	school	school	school	school	z–z–z–	z–z–z–
8:00	school	school	school	school	school	Bkfast	Bkfast
9:00	school	school	school	school	school	soccer	church
11:00	school	school	school	school	school	family time	free time
3:30	**practice**	soccer	**practice**	chess club	**practice**	read, play	free time
4:00	piano lesson	soccer	homework	chess club	homework	**practice**	**practice**
5:00	homework	**practice**	free time	chess club	free time	read, play	free time
6:00	dinner	dinner	dinner	dinner	dinner	read, play	dinner
7:00	homework	homework	homework	homework	homework	dinner	homework
8:00	read	read	read	homework	read	movie	read, play
10:00	bed	bed	bed	bed	bed	bed	bed

This is the schedule of someone whose goal is to practice an hour a day. Tuesday, the day after the lesson, contains 90 minutes of possible practice time, and Thursday is a day off; all other days contain 60 minutes of practice time.

For an adult the schedule would look quite different. The important thing is to create an accurate picture of your week and to include specific times for practicing each day.

Avoid the temptation to push all or most of your practicing into the weekends. Your physical skills will improve faster if you use them every day. It's a good idea to take one day off a week, to enjoy the frequent sensation of a fresh start.

Post your schedule near the piano. Try it for a month. Make changes if you need to, but once you are satisfied with the schedule, stick to it. If you take your schedule seriously and use this book regularly, your practicing will become more interesting, more enjoyable, and far more effective.

USING THIS BOOK

There are as many ways to practice as there are pieces to play. The practice tips that follow (identified by names in **bold italics**) can be used as written, in combination with each other or modified to suit your particular needs. They can be used in any order, on any piece they fit, wherever you think they will help. Pick a few tips that suit your needs today. Tomorrow try something different. Over time you will learn to select the practice tips that best fit each musical problem, and you will develop your own favorites. But whenever you need a change, you will still have a variety of other practice options to choose from.

If you are smart about the way you start practicing, you will learn faster and better and have a more satisfying experience from beginning to end.

Chapter 1 shows how to set yourself up for success. Follow these guidelines for examining the printed page, and discover how much you can learn about a piece by mapping it before you ever sit down at the piano. Chapter 2 explains how to play your piece for the first time without starting any bad habits. Chapter 3 helps you organize what you've learned up to this point, so that you can plan the most effective strategy for practicing your piece.

CHAPTER 1
MAPPING THE COURSE

Imagine you are taking a cross-country hike. You could just set off and start trudging. Or you could sit down with a map and determine where the longest, steepest hills are, where the terrain is easy or challenging, where to stop for lunch, what kind of equipment you might need, and how long the hike may take.

Turn the printed page of your music into a map. It can make your practice path easier and keep you headed in the right direction from the first practice session right through memorization and performance.

Map every new piece that you intend to study seriously. Some mapping tasks are simple and take only a few minutes, others take longer. Investing 30 or 40 minutes to map a new piece will make all your subsequent practicing more efficient and rewarding.

And remember, you start using a map *before* taking a hike, so map your piece before practicing it.

SIGNPOSTS

A musical score is packed with signs that tell you what and how to play. These signs are called notation. They provide all kinds of information about the music that will guide you along your way. But standard music notation is not always user-friendly: some of its symbols are difficult to read, others have hidden meanings. Jotting notes to yourself and inserting visual aids will ease the mental strain you may feel later when you have to translate all these symbols into sound. Do write in your music, just as you would jot notes on a map—to circle your destination, for example, or mark the turns you need to make. Write in pencil, though, not pen. Mistakes happen, and when they do you want to be able to correct them easily.

Some things don't need to be written but should be carefully noted—the key signature and the time signature, for example. You will need to mark any flats and sharps that might trip you up and write in some measure numbers, finger numbers, and word definitions. When it's time to practice the piece, having these signposts stand out on the page will make your trip easier.

Key and Time Signatures

At the beginning of your piece you will find a key signature and a time signature. From the key signature, determine the key of the piece and write it under the first measure. If you see any key changes later in the piece, label them. If the key signature has more sharps or flats than you are used to, pencil in the sharp or flat signs to the left of any notes they belong to.

Next, circle the time signature and remind yourself of its meaning: the top number shows how many counts each measure contains; the bottom number indicates what kind of note gets a count.

Accidentals

Wherever you find an accidental, search the rest of the measure to catch any repeats of it. For example, suppose you have an F♯ at the beginning of a measure on the treble clef top line. Run your finger (or something smaller, like a pencil) along that line all the way to the end of the measure. If you bump into another F, write a ♯ sign to the left of it.

Measure Numbers

If your piece doesn't have printed measure numbers, write in a measure number at the beginning of each line of music. You'll use these numbers later to stay on track as you compare different sections of the piece.

Fingering

Pieces often contain printed fingering in a tricky section. But if that section is repeated later in the piece, it probably appears without fingering. This omission can be treacherous because you may accidentally use a different fingering the second time, which will not only make it harder to learn but may also cause problems when you memorize the piece. So if you see printed fingering in one part of your piece, copy that fingering into all the identical parts.

Vocabulary

Most musical scores contain directions for the performer, but the words may be in Italian, or another language, instead of English. Music dictionaries carry definitions of all musical terms, whatever language they come from. Always look up unfamiliar words: they are messages from the composer. Don't overlook the title and the tempo indication (usually found just above the first measure of the piece). Write the definitions directly into your music.

LANDMARKS

A map gives you an idea of what to expect along a certain route. Once you've studied the map, you know what landmarks to look for, what obstacles to avoid, which path to follow at each turn. Study your score just as carefully, so that you will be fully prepared for your musical trip.

First look at the big picture to get a general idea of the overall structure, or form, of your piece. Understanding the form will help you organize your practicing.

Once you have identified the form of the piece, compare one section with another to find out what material is repeated, or nearly repeated. Within each section you will look for familiar patterns—scales and arpeggios, for example—that you already know how to play. And then you need to search for any complicated-looking rhythm pattern, so that you can write in the counts before you even begin practicing. Finally, you will give special attention to the piece's harmonic structure by writing in the chords you recognize. All of these landmarks, once noted in your score, will make the terrain seem less daunting when you start practicing the piece.

The Big Picture

Look at the big picture first. (If your piece is a contrapuntal piece from the Baroque period, see box "The Big Picture Baroque Style," p. 14.)

Go through the piece and search for large contrasting sections. Most pieces, even long ones, have two or three major sections. Label each one with a capital letter. Use the same letter (*A...A*) for like sections. Use different letters (*A...B*) for contrasting sections.

Contrasting sections of a piece usually look different enough on the page that you can recognize them immediately. If the section divisions of your piece aren't obvious to you, look at the first few measures and then try to find the same material later in the piece. Gradually you will see patterns emerge, probably into one of the following forms:

Ternary (*ABA*). Duncombe's Fanfare in C Major (fig. 1.1) contains three sections. The first and third parts look the same, and the middle part looks different. So we label the sections *ABA* and call the form ternary. A piece in ternary form could contain repeats within a section or contrasting phrases within a section (as in fig. 1.1). This *A* section contains two contrasting phrases, and the *B* section is one long phrase made up of sequences. We would still label the piece *ABA* or ternary form.

Fig. 1.1. Duncombe, Fanfare in C Major.

FANFARE IN C MAJOR

William Duncombe

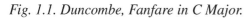

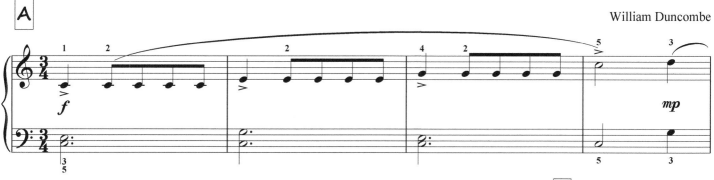

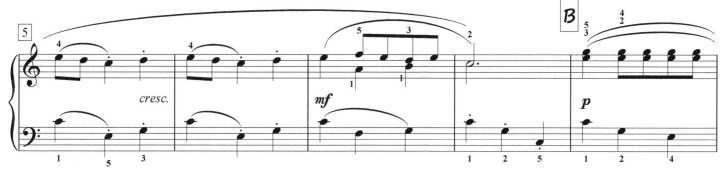

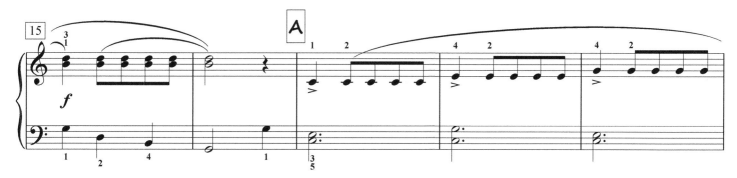

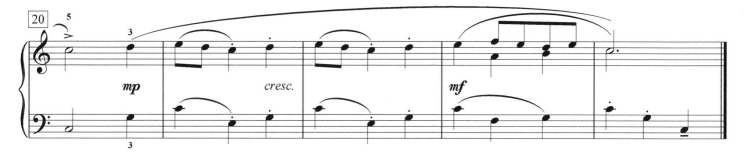

Binary (AB). Figure 1.2 shows a two-part structure with the second section roughly equal in length to the first, but very clearly different from it. This is labeled *AB* and called binary form. Notice that both the *A* and *B* sections contain two phrases—phrases that start out the same but end differently.

Fig. 1.2. Beethoven, Russian Folk Song, Op. 107, No. 3.

RUSSIAN FOLK SONG, OP. 107, NO. 3

Beethoven

Rounded Binary (ABa). Rounded binary is like binary *(AB)*, but with a shortened form of the *A* section added before the end. For example, if the original *A* section is eight measures long, the final *A* section might be only four measures long. We use a lower case *a* to show that the return of *A* is shortened, and we label the piece *ABa* (fig. 1.3).

Fig. 1.3. Hook, Minuetto.

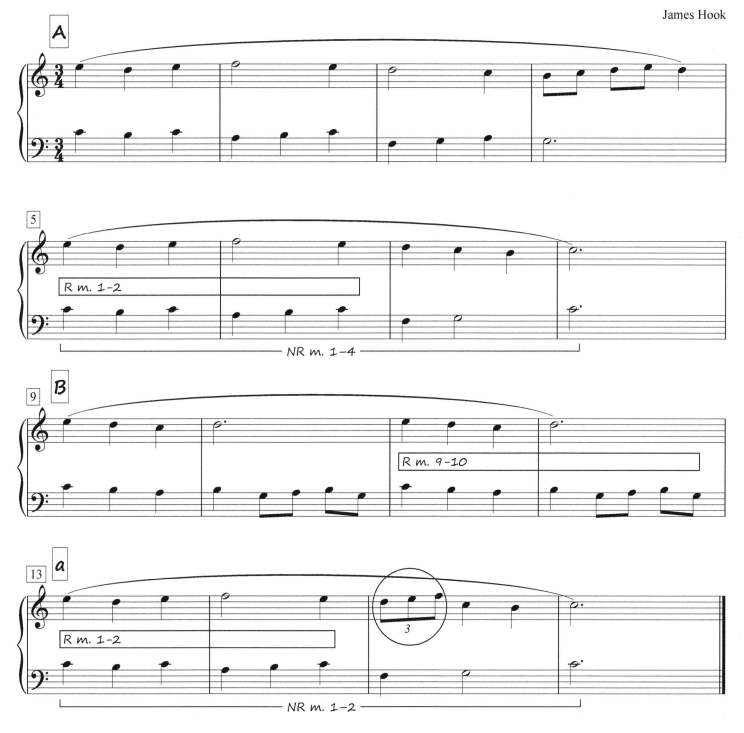

MINUETTO

James Hook

THE BIG PICTURE BAROQUE STYLE

Much of the music of the Baroque era is written entirely in counterpoint or what we call contrapuntal style, meaning a musical texture of two or more independent lines or voices. If your piece is a Baroque composition in contrapuntal style, you need a special strategy to analyze the piece. The process described below fits a Bach invention, sinfonia, or fugue perfectly and can be adapted to fit Bach's *Little Preludes* or any Baroque dance form.

In a contrapuntal piece, the main theme is called the subject—like the subject of a painting or the main character in a story. (The terms "subject" and "counter subject" may strictly speaking refer only to fugues, but I find them useful on other contrapuntal forms as well.) To understand how a contrapuntal piece is put together, you will need to identify various statements of the subject and the counter subject. In addition, look for and label examples of episodes, sequence, and imitation.

The *subject* is the melody that begins the piece. Its length could be anywhere from a few beats to several measures. In an invention, sinfonia, or fugue, you will know the subject is over when a second voice enters. The subject will reappear several times during the piece as it does in the fragment from the Bach Invention No. 1, below. Find each subject in your piece. Mark it with a bracket and a label: an S (subject) followed by a number, like S1, S2, S3, etc. You may find small changes from one subject to the next. Circle the changes. Write in the key of each one.

J.S. Bach, Invention No. 1.

The *counter subject* (CS) is the melody that accompanies the subject. It is similar to a minor character in a story or a figure in the background of a painting.

Episodes are sections of the piece that have no subject. Mark the episodes: *E1*, *E2*, etc. Notice what motifs are used in each episode. Play each episode.

Baroque music contains less exact repetition than the music of later periods, but *sequence* and *imitation* (p. 15) are common. Mark any examples that you find.

Comparisons

Pieces usually contain elements that resemble each other to a greater or lesser degree. Search through your piece to find and label examples of repetition, near repetition, sequence, and imitation.

Repetition. Label identical motifs, measures, or phrases with an *R* for *repeat*. Composers typically repeat motifs, measures, phrases, and even entire sections of a piece. Recognizing such repeats can save you a lot of work, since you won't need to practice them—especially repeats of entire sections—until you are ready to put the whole piece together. Once you've labeled all the repeats, you will find you have much less to practice!

For example in the Hook Minuetto (fig. 1.3), measures 5–6 and 13–14 are exact repeats of measures 1–2; measures 11–12 repeat measures 9–10 and measure 16 is a repeat of measure 8. Marking the repeats makes it clear that 7 of 16 measures—or almost half of the piece—do not need to be practiced.

Near Repetition. When you are labeling repeating elements, watch for small changes and label them *NR* for *near repetition*. In figure 1.3, for example, measures 5–8 are identical to measures 13–16, with one tiny exception: the first beat of measure 15, right hand. Such small changes can cause big trouble later—trouble like habitual stumbles and memory lapses. Always circle a spot like this, and plan to pay special attention to it throughout the whole process of practicing and memorizing the piece. Figure 1.3 shows a circled spot (measure 15) in a near repeat (*NR*).

Sequence. A sequence is a series of motifs or phrases that contain identical intervals but different pitches (fig. 1.4). Label sequences with an *Sq* for *sequence*. Because each motif contains different notes, you will still have to practice them all. But recognizing how much they have in common will make practicing them easier.

Fig. 1.4. Schein, Allemande.

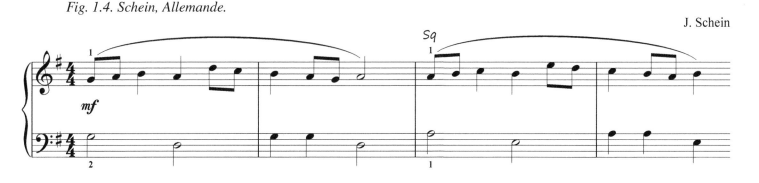

J. Schein

Imitation. If a musical idea is repeated exactly, except that it's placed in a different octave, we call it imitation. Label this kind of repeat *I* for *imitation*.

Familiar Elements
You probably can play many scales, chords, and arpeggios automatically without thinking much about the notes and fingering. Search for these old friends in your piece, and label them so that a quick glance will tell you what to play. Not only will these passages instantly become easier, you may also find that you can memorize them on the spot. Since you already know the notes and fingering, all you have to remember is where and how they occur in your piece.

Be careful, though: scale patterns in a piece can fool you. Scales don't always occur exactly the way that you practice them. In figure 1.5, for example, Clementi writes two scales, one from G to G and the next from B to B. The first is indeed a G major scale, but the second is not a B major scale, because it has only one sharp. Think of both these scales, then, as being in G major but starting and ending on different notes.

The scale in measure 1 is marked G with a rising arrow representing an ascending scale. The scale in measure 3 has the same mark with (*B-B*) added. This means that the scale is in the key of G but it starts and ends on B.

Fig. 1.5. Clementi, Sonatina, Op. 36, No. 1.

Clementi

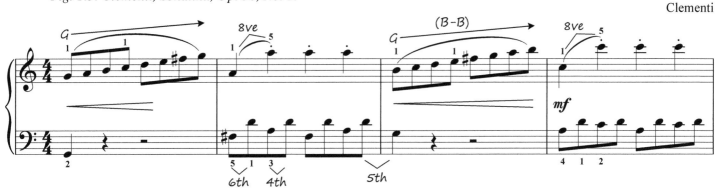

Composers use this technique a lot —imagine how boring music would be if every G scale in every G major piece started and ended on G. Understanding this, and examining scales carefully when you begin practicing a new piece, will help you learn them easily and without error.

If you don't immediately recognize a skip, especially if you have to count lines and spaces, take the time to label the interval (fig. 1.5, measures 2 and 4).

Composers also construct scales combining fragments of regular (diatonic) scales with fragments of chromatic scales. Mark chromatic fragments with a bracket, a *CH* as in figure 1.6, or make up your own symbol.

Fig. 1.6. Chopin, Waltz, Op. 64, No. 2.

Chopin

Rhythm

You are probably familiar with most of the rhythm patterns you see in your piece. But if you see a rhythm pattern that only happens once or that looks confusing, you have found a potential trouble spot. Stop and write in the counts. Simply writing in the counts may solve the mystery. Draw the numbers in the space between treble and bass clefs and line up each number with the note that falls on its count. If there are eighth notes or sixteenth notes, divide the counts by using "and" (&). When all the numbers seem to be in the right place, check your math. The number of counts you have written in the measure should match the top number of the piece's time signature.

Chord Labels

- Label any chords that you recognize. They could be block chords or broken chords. Put each label underneath the bass clef notes it describes.

- Label the chords only when they change.

- Skip any chords you don't recognize.

Reading chords is much more difficult than reading single notes. If you label familiar chords before practicing a piece you will recognize them more easily and be more likely to play them correctly. This does take time at the beginning, but it saves time later on. Labeling forces you to examine a chord note by note, which is the best way to get it right the first time. And seeing that chord label in the score will help you learn it faster, remember it longer, and realize that something is amiss if a finger lands on a wrong note and changes the chord. Suppose you've written a capital *D* under a particular spot. One day you play an F natural by mistake. Your ear tells you, "Stop! That should sound major, but it sounded minor."

When labeling familiar chords, use symbols that fit your own knowledge of harmony. Use capital letters for major or augmented chords and lowercase letters for minor or diminished chords (see fig. 1.7). If you wish, add a number to show the chord's inversion. Or you can use Roman numerals and figured bass. Just be sure to use symbols that you can instantly translate into action.

Fig. 1.7. Tchaikovsky, In an Old Russian Church.

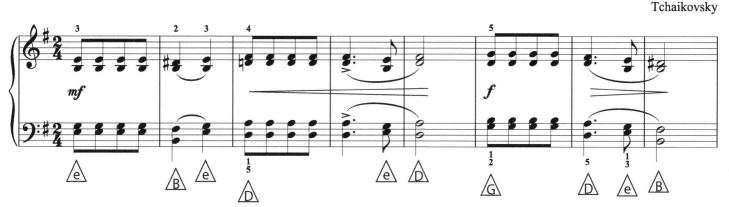

CHAPTER 2
FIRST STEPS AT THE PIANO

You have discovered much about your piece from studying the score. Now it's time to put that knowledge to work at the piano.

This is a dangerous moment. The natural inclination is to jump in and start playing, hands together, and at something approaching final tempo. But remember that your ears and your fingers are about to form their first aural/physical impression of the piece. And first impressions last, even though sometimes we wish they wouldn't. Your ears will send the new sounds to your brain, which is brilliant at grabbing and holding new ideas. Your fingers have muscle memory—you can count on them to remember and repeat what they do in the first play-through. If you miss notes and scramble rhythms now or if you slow down or speed up the pulse here and there, you can bet these errors will come back to haunt you.

It is crucial, then, to start a piece *slowly*. Never try to play up to speed the first time. Take a moment to consider everything you know about the piece from mapping the score. Ask yourself, what tempo might get me through the piece without a single stumble? Set the metronome at that speed. If you stay in control, you know you've found the right tempo. If you trip up, reduce the speed. Take time out to *breathe* and *think* periodically. Continuity is not important at this stage—avoiding mistakes is.

Here are some strategies to help you succeed from the start. Use some or all of these practice tips instead of simply playing through the piece.

All Alone

A good way to do the first play-through without forming bad habits is to play one element at a time, so that you don't have to think of everything at once.

- Play one hand alone, and then the other.

- Play the melody alone. The melody might be in the right hand or the left hand, or it might switch from one to the other.

- Play the accompaniment alone. (You've already labeled many chords, so that will help.)

- Play the whole piece without rhythm: Give all notes equal value as if every single one were, for example, a half note. Use the metronome for company, set around 60, or you can play it without the metronome.

Relaxation

The first play-through of a piece sometimes brings on mental and physical tension, which can sabotage your efforts. Playing slowly helps, but staying slow is not always easy. To help you play *adagio*, drop and lift your wrist on each beat. This movement takes time, so it will help you avoid speeding, which in turn will keep you from tensing up under the pressure of playing new material. Tension leads you into errors, relaxation leads you away from them.

As you play, let the distinctive sound of each harmony fill your ears. Keep looking ahead to avoid surprises. If you see something puzzling in the next measure, stop and examine it before going on. The goal here is to fully enjoy the new sounds without tensing up and without making any mistakes.

Clumping

Clump the notes of one measure, or half measure, into a single large chord or cluster (fig. 2.1). Slowly and softly, play each cluster until it feels and sounds comfortable. This is a good way to start becoming familiar with the keyboard geography of your piece—in other words, to get the feel of the notes into your hand.

Fig. 2.1. Tchaikovsky, The Sick Doll.

Note: Throughout this book, practice tip names are indicated by ***bold italics***.

Slice & Dice Voices

If your piece, or any part of your piece, requires you to play two voices (also called lines) in one hand, treat each line as a separate entity from the earliest stage of practicing right through performance. If you are not sure which notes belong to which voice, check the direction of each note stem. The notes with up stems belong to one voice, and the notes with down stems belong to another.

Try the following steps on the example from J.S. Bach (fig. 2.2) There are three lines of music, one in the treble clef and two in the bass clef. Imagine this music being sung by three singers—soprano (S), tenor (T), and bass (B).

Fig. 2.2. J.S. Bach, Anglaise from French Suite 3.

Bach

1. Play each voice separately, with one hand. Use any fingering as long as it allows you to play legato.

2. Play two voices together, with two hands, in every possible combination: ST, SB, BT.

3. Study the bass clef lines, decide what fingering to use, and write in a finger number for every note.

4. Play both tenor and bass voices with the left hand, as written. Can you still hear two distinct melodies?

5. Add the right hand and play all three voices together, as written, six times.

Although this example is by Bach, all composers use counterpoint at times, so learn to recognize it and always give it this special treatment.

Ottline

This tip gets its name from Margaret Saunders Ott, who taught her students to use it on a brand new piece, or when memorizing a piece, or when preparing a piece for performance.

Use a pencil to draw a line from above the treble staff straight down through the bass clef on each beat of the measure (see fig. 2.3). (Notice the patterns revealed by these lines: a C Major triad outline, m. 1–2, and a G dominant seventh chord outline, m. 5–6.)

Fig. 2.3. Lynes, Sonatina in C.

Play through the piece, but play only the notes on the lines. Play softly and non-legato. As you play the notes on one line, look ahead to the next one. Move gently and smoothly from one line to another.

Ottline Quickie

Use this tip to learn a piece in a very short time.

In a section or an entire piece, first play only the notes that fall on the downbeats. Play again, this time adding whatever notes fall on the second most important beat of each measure. For example, if the piece is in 4/4 time, play the first and third beats. Next, add either the second or fourth beat, then the "ands" between beats. Continue this routine until you are playing all the notes in every measure.

CHAPTER 3
FORMULATING PRACTICE STRATEGIES

Now that you've had the pleasure of playing through your piece, you may be tempted to play it again and again and again, today, tomorrow, and for days, weeks, or months until the piece is "learned." But that kind of repetition may lead you into bad habits—wrong notes, wrong rhythms, maybe even a measure left out or played in the wrong clef, and so on.

Rather than starting down the path of mindless repetition, think over what you learned from your play-through. For example, you might say to yourself:

> Some parts are easy: I could probably sightread them up to tempo.
> Some of the notes are too high, or too low, to read easily.
> I fumbled the fingering in the B section.
> I might have left out a rest somewhere.
> There are too many accidentals in that fourth phrase.
> The left-hand part is really hard.
> I am not sure how to count the third line.

Use these clues to plan your practice. For example:

Some parts are easy: I probably could sightread them up to tempo. All right, then you can postpone practicing these parts until later. Don't waste your practice time playing the easy parts over and over. (What you might do, however, is reward yourself *after* a good practice session by playing through the easy parts as often as you like.)

Some notes are too high, or too low, to read easily. The best strategy here is to deal with the problem as soon as you see it. First get a pencil. Then figure out what the notes are by counting leger lines one by one in thirds: FACEG up from the top treble line or GECAF down from the bottom bass line (remember these as "Face-G" and "G-caf"). Write one or two note names as guideposts, but don't label every one. Occasional letters will catch your eye and help you find the notes, but a letter on every note may become a meaningless blur and therefore of no help at all.

I fumbled the fingering in the B section. Make a note to use the **10-Step Finger Guide** (Chapter 5) and to write a number over or under every note in the passage that bothered you.

I might have left out a rest somewhere. Leaving out rests, especially at the end of a phrase or a section (fig. 3.1), is a common mistake, so be glad that you noticed. Here again the best strategy is to mark the problem spot immediately. Write in the count of the rest measure plus a few measures before and after it. Plan to practice this part separately from the rest of the piece, slowly and counting aloud.

Fig. 3.1. Mozart, Sonata K545.

Mozart

There are too many accidentals in that fourth phrase. Accidentals look intimidating and that makes us want to avoid them. Be brave! Put a note in your music to pay special attention to this phrase from day one of practicing until the difficulties disappear.

The left-hand part is really hard. Resolve to be patient, to practice the left hand part alone every day and not to play hands together at all until you're completely comfortable playing the left hand alone.

I am not sure how to count the third line. Try writing in the count. If you cannot decipher the rhythm—and this does happen sometimes—leave it out (***All Alone***, Chapter 2). Practicing it this way will get you started learning the notes, and then you can ask your teacher for help at the next lesson. It's better to leave out the rhythm than to practice it wrong.

PART II

THE EARLY STAGES OF PRACTICING

Now that you have mapped your piece and tried it out at the piano, it's time to begin the actual practicing.

Tackling a new piece can feel overwhelming. You may worry about how long the piece is, how much there is to learn, how many hours it will take, how hard it will be. Stressful thoughts like these can drain enjoyment from the early stages of practicing. Read Chapter 4 for help in organizing your practice, suggestions on what to do first, and strategies that work best when beginning to practice a new piece.

Chapter 5 addresses the important issue of comfort at the keyboard: overall body comfort in terms of general position and mobility, the hand comfort that good fingering brings, and peace of mind through techniques for avoiding practice anxiety.

Chapter 6 offers tips on playing accurately from the beginning and on dealing with any mistakes that may crop up despite your best efforts.

Once the basics are in place, consult Chapter 7 for tips on building fluency and Chapter 8 for putting meaning into the music.

Now is the time to think small. Keep the PACT (see Introduction) in mind. In particular, remember *patience*: don't expect miracles. Remember *tunnel vision*: focus on one thing at a time. And do congratulate yourself every day for even the smallest signs of progress.

CHAPTER 4
GETTING ORGANIZED

This chapter offers suggestions for structuring early practice sessions: step-by-step plans, ideas on how to divide the work, and procedures you can use to maintain interest and improve efficiency.

Take small bites—work on one part of the piece at a time, one hand at a time. What makes a small bite will vary from one piece to the next. It could be as little as one measure, it could be an entire phrase. You'll have to decide.

Keep in mind that playing slowly gives your brain time to process everything. The metronome makes a good practice partner because it keeps you from speeding up unintentionally.

If you stumble even once on any task, stop and mark the spot in your music to help you avoid making the same mistake again. You can use a pencil, a highlighter, colored tape, stickers, little drawings—anything that catches your eye.

The first two practice tips, **Back Up** and **Make a Date**, are based on one of the most powerful precepts in this book: begin at the end, not the beginning. When you read a book, of course you start on page one and read to the end. Similarly, when you sight-read a piece of music—that is, when you play it through just for fun or to get a sense of how it sounds—you start on measure one and play to the end. Not surprisingly, people usually set out to "learn" a piece in the same way, by starting at the beginning.

It's not an effective learning method, though. Typically, a person only gets through a few measures before having to stop and start again. The second time through more measures may get covered but, oops, another breakdown and back to the beginning again. This pattern may recur a dozen times or more before the end of the piece is reached. And the same thing may happen every day for weeks or even months.

Practicing this way means that the most repeated, and therefore the best learned, part of a piece is the beginning. And it means that the playing gets weaker and weaker as it goes along, with the worst part at the end.

Yet very few pieces are most difficult at the beginning. In fact the final section of a piece is often much harder than the rest of the piece, even if only because it is different from the rest of the piece. And no one wants to end poorly. We'd like to end with a flourish, with confidence, with a feeling of excitement. Too often it's just the opposite.

Back Up

Start practicing a piece or part of a piece at the end instead of the beginning. Try out this idea on the excerpt from the Bach Prelude in figure 4.1, and then apply it to your own piece.

Fig. 4.1. J.S. Bach, Prelude in D Minor.

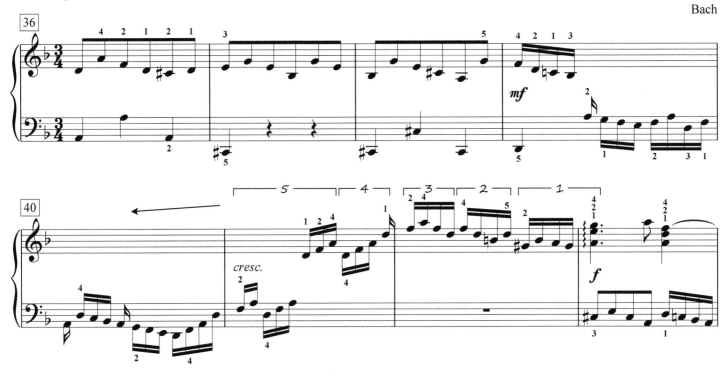

1. Decide how many notes you can handle at one time. This could be anything from less than a measure to a whole section of the piece: it depends on how difficult the passage seems to you. Mark each fragment with a bracket.

2. Number each bracket, beginning at the end.

3. Write a finger number over the first note of each fragment. Make sure this fits the fingering in the previous measure. Otherwise you may waste time by practicing with fingering that will have to be changed later.

4. Play bracket #1 perfectly four times.

5. Play bracket #2 perfectly four times.

6. Play brackets #2 and #1 together until they feel easy.

7. Continue working backwards, adding one fragment at a time until you reach the beginning of the challenge passage (measure 39 in this example) and can play the whole thing smoothly from beginning to end. Then repeat it several times for reinforcement.

8. Start several measures before the difficult passage, and play through to the end. When perfect, repeat four more times.

Make a Date

Before you begin practicing a long piece, decide how much material you can cover each day. The amount will depend on the piece—you might be able to cover three or four phrases a day in a Clementi sonatina or Mozart sonata. But if you're working on a Bach prelude or minuet or invention, a single measure or two might be plenty for one day's work.

Starting from the end of the piece, pick out the material you plan to cover in your first practice session and write today's date on it. Put tomorrow's date on the section before that. Continue until you reach the beginning of the piece and have entered a date for the completion of every section.

This will help you keep from feeling overwhelmed. Stick to your schedule by completing each day's work on time.

Connections

Reading music is complicated. Your eyes look at the page, gather information, and send it to your brain, which makes calculations and relays the message to your fingers, which then play the notes.

Usually it is easy to tell at a glance which right-hand notes or rests go with which left hand notes or rests. Sometimes, though, a passage may look so odd that you can't tell what goes together. Figure 4.2, for example, shows a measure where both hands are busy, but actually play together only twice—on the first and the third counts. Put connection lines on those beats to eliminate guesswork about which notes belong together.

Fig. 4.2. J.S. Bach, March in D Major.

Same/Similar

Find a short section, phrase, or motif that occurs more than once in your piece. Count how many times it returns. Is it exactly the same each time? If so, you can take all but one of these sections out of your practice plan.

If a section does change slightly, what exactly is the difference? Should you do something to highlight the change?

- A melody could contain the same intervals each time but start on a different note, as in figure 4.3. You could show this by using rising dynamics on each measure: *piano—mezzo piano—mezzo forte,* or for a stronger contrast, *piano—mezzo forte—forte.*

- A melody could start on the same note each time but use different intervals, as in figure 4.4. Here it would be nice to emphasize each changing note with a tenuto or small accent.

- It could have the same rhythm but different notes (fig. 4.5). This big of a change will never go unnoticed, but you could still enhance it with dynamics.

- It could start the same but end differently (fig. 4.6). Notice that, although the melody is exactly the same through the middle of measure 3, Beethoven surprises us by changing the harmony from G major (m. 1) to E minor (m. 3). Be sure to consider this harmonic change when deciding how to shape this phrase.

Fig. 4.3. Beethoven, Sonatina in G Major.

Beethoven

Fig. 4.4. Kuhlau, Scotch Dance in B♭ Major.

Kuhlau

Fig. 4.5. Tchaikovsky, Waltz.

Tchaikovsky

Fig. 4.6. Beethoven, Sonatina in G Major.

Beethoven

Songlines
Make up words to help you learn and remember the notes.

For example, for figure 4.3 you could sing,

Skip up to A,

then up to C,

then pause on E.

Or for figure 4.4:

Up an 8th,

then a 7th,

then a 6th,

then a 5th,

then a 4th,

then we turn around and come to rest on B.

CHAPTER 5
GETTING COMFORTABLE

You can't play the piano without using some physical tension. Muscles must work so that your arm can carry the hand, so that your hand can support your fingers, so that your fingers can enter the keys. But too much tension, or the wrong kind of tension, is dangerous. Tension can prevent you from playing fast, make your sound harsh, and cause discomfort, pain, or permanent injury.

Make a fist. Open your hand but keep it hard. Try playing something fast on the piano. Not only is it practically impossible to play this way, but you will immediately feel some discomfort in your forearm or elbow. This is a good demonstration of how tension keeps us from moving freely and how easily tension can hurt us.

Another obstacle is mental tension caused by those little worries that accumulate when we are working on a long or complicated task.

This chapter addresses physical and mental tension of both kinds, with advice on how to manage them. And there are tips on rhythm and fingering, including a detailed guide to help pianists find the best fingering.

POSITION AND MOBILITY AT THE KEYBOARD

Pianists often forget to think about position at the instrument—how to sit so that they can cover the entire keyboard easily. Physical comfort greatly influences the quality and rate of development of a pianist's technique. It is also essential to healthy practicing. Poor posture and other tics may lead to injury. If you ever experience pain during practicing, consult your teacher immediately. It is never a good idea to play through pain.

Starting Lineup
Use this checklist to set yourself up at the keyboard.

- Keep space between your waist and your elbows—don't hug yourself! Each arm needs to be able to move freely over at least half the keyboard without bumping into your body.

- Sit far enough away from the keyboard so that your elbows are slightly in front of your body when your hands are on the keyboard.

- Sit high enough so that when your fingers are in playing position there is a flat plane from your elbows to the knuckles at the top of your fingers.

- Sit tall in the front half of the bench so that your weight pulls you forward, not back.

- Rest both heels on the floor unless you are using the pedal. Crossed legs cause the body to tilt backwards or slouch, which makes it harder to utilize body weight when you need a big sound. Slouching also has psychological consequences. It can affect your mental state, dulling your energy. Sitting tall with the support of a strong back makes you feel more alert and energetic.

Good Moves
The piano keyboard is four feet wide, so sooner or later your hands have to move some distance away from the center. They must have support as they travel. The torso and upper arms should act as a conveyor belt to carry the hands where they need to go.

- Move your torso and arms from side to side behind your hands.

- Move from the hips and waist while remaining seated in the center of the bench.

- Keep your chest open and your shoulders sloping. Playing with lifted shoulders can cause muscle strain.

- If your hand needs to cover a great distance, carry it with your upper arm instead of sticking your hand out to the side on its own. You can experience this kind of arm movement by doing a glissando. Move the same way, with the arm carrying the hand, for a big arpeggio or a long scale.

BASIC MATH

What could be more important to music than rhythm? Music loses its meaning without rhythm. A familiar melody deprived of its rhythm can be completely unrecognizable. Test this by playing the following example for a friend or parent:

Did they recognize it? Probably not. Put the rhythm back and play it again—it should be recognized this time.

Rhythm is something that we feel deeply. Regular, toe-tapping rhythmic patterns bring satisfaction to performer and listener alike. And once a rhythm pattern is learned, it stays with us. If the rhythm is learned wrong, correcting it takes a lot of work, and the spot always remains uncomfortable and vulnerable to error or memory slip. That's why it's so important to do your music math correctly from the start.

If you understand basic note values and how they relate to each other, you can solve any rhythm problem. Most music math problems can be solved by mentally dividing each main beat into smaller note values and setting the metronome to tick once for each small note. But you also need to make rhythm physical. Tap it, step it, clap it, but above all, count it out loud.

Counting aloud, or vocal counting, is our most powerful tool for mastering rhythms, in fact it's often the best way to solve a rhythm problem. This is because vocal counting resonates both internally and externally—unlike a metronome, for example, which you hear only externally. When you count aloud you not only hear the sounds externally but you also feel them internally, because of the vibrations your vocal chords set in motion inside your body. That is why you will find the words "count aloud" so often in this book.

Tap Tap

Large muscle movements are easier to coordinate than small muscle movements, which is why it is smart to tap out a difficult rhythm (using whole arm movement) before trying to play it on the piano (using only finger movement).

1. Turn the metronome on. If the rhythm is complicated—made up of several different types of notes—set the tick to the smallest note value. Now tap the rhythm, hands alone and then hands together, while counting aloud. (If you stumble the least bit, write in the counting.) Tap with a flat hand, moving your whole forearm from the elbow on each tap.

2. Play the right-hand part while tapping the left-hand part.

3. Play the left-hand part while tapping the right-hand part.

4. Play hands together while counting aloud.

Rest Action

Don't rest on rests: move on rests! When you see a rest, lift your wrist just enough to bring your fingers slightly out of the keys. Let your hand hover above the keys like a little helicopter during the rest, dropping into the next note when it's time. If the next note is far away, use the rest to travel to the new position.

Over and Over

When one musical idea, or motif, is repeated many times, it's easy to lose track of the repetitions and play too many or too few. A notorious example occurs in Beethoven's *Für Elise* (fig. 5.1).

Fig. 5.1. Beethoven, Für Elise.

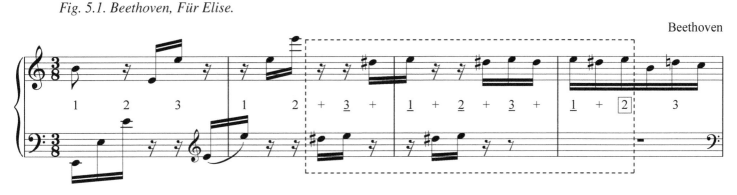

The only way to be sure you are playing this passage correctly is to know not only how many times to repeat the pattern (D♯ to E), but also exactly when the repetitions end and the next idea begins.

In Für Elise the pattern occurs six times. D♯ always leads into E, like a miniature upbeat and downbeat. This happens on each of the underlined counts; the pattern changes on the boxed count.

Use visual aids to learn patterns like this, and always begin counting at least one measure before the repetitions begin. Count the patterns and then count the beats.

Rhythm Bridges

A sudden change in a piece's rhythm pattern can disturb your sense of the pulse. Such changes are common in Classical period pieces such as the sonatina in figure 5.2. At first there is a note on every eighth-note count, but then suddenly the pattern changes into sixteenth notes. Try the following steps on this example, then on your own piece.

Fig. 5.2. Kuhlau, Sonatina, Op. 55, No. 3.

1. Mark each place where an established rhythm pattern changes.

2. With the metronome set at a comfortable speed, play two measures of the old rhythm pattern plus two measures of the new rhythm pattern five times perfectly while counting aloud.

3. Repeat step 2 without the metronome but still counting aloud.

4. Do step 3, this time counting to yourself.

5. Turn the metronome on again and play with it. Does it sound the same as step 3 and 4? If so, you are finished for the day.

6. Do this exercise every day for a week.

FINDING AND USING GOOD FINGERING

The eminent American pianist and scholar Charles Rosen was once asked, "What is the first thing you do with a new piece?" His answer was, "I just put in the fingering."[1] If a major artist who has concertized around the world starts by writing in the fingering, shouldn't we be doing it, too?

When composers or editors or teachers put fingering in the score, they do it to make our lives easier. They want to help us play comfortably and accurately and, when necessary, fast. Yet many students ignore printed fingering or fingering written in by their teachers and would never consider writing in fingering themselves. Instead they play along with no particular plan in mind, using whatever finger falls into place.

But random fingering can cause wrong notes, crooked rhythms, messy articulation, bumpy melodies, and memory lapses. So if your piece contains printed fingering, follow it. If the given fingering seems awkward and you think you have a better solution, pencil in your idea and ask your teacher's opinion at the next lesson.

If your new piece has no fingering, just follow Charles Rosen's example—put in the fingering. Use the finger guide below to find the best solution and stick to it faithfully unless a change is absolutely necessary.

10-Step Finger Guide

Most parts of a piece will be easy to finger, and the more difficult passages usually include fingering suggestions from the composer or editor. When you need to create a fingering plan yourself, follow these steps.

1. Play a phrase, or a part of it, hands alone at a slow speed. Use whatever printed finger numbers you see in the music and fill in the gaps with the implied fingering. If you are familiar with standard scale and arpeggio fingering, use that knowledge. Choose fingering that fits your hand and that feels comfortable. Do not use the same finger twice in a row in a legato melody. If you do, you will destroy the legato.

2. If you see more than one way to finger the passage, try each one at least five times. Choose the one that feels most comfortable and suits the music best.

3. Play the notes under each long slur in your piece. Make sure that your fingering for that passage results in a legato line.

4. Look at staccato or non-legato passages and at breaks between slurs. In such spots you are free to move your hand from one position to another, so you don't have to use legato fingering. Don't move around any more than necessary, however. The simpler your moves are, the easier it will be to play fluently.

5. If you can't figure out how to finger a passage, search for the one spot that can only be fingered one way. Write in that fingering, and work backward or forward from there.

6. Choose fingering that helps you play musically. For example, avoid using weak combinations, like 4–5 or 3–4–5, at climaxes. Instead use finger 2 or 3, or even the thumb if that works, so that you can show the high point of the phrase easily.

[1] *Clavier Magazine*, November 1999, Vol. 38, No. 9.

7. Make the fingering as comfortable as possible. Chopin used to teach the B major scale first, because it is the most comfortable one to play. The B major scale feels good because we use our longer fingers—2, 3, and 4—on the black keys (which are further away) and our shorter fingers—pinky and thumb—on the white keys (which are closer). Remember this when choosing fingering.

8. When you feel you have the best solution, test it by playing small bits of the passage up to tempo. Don't think that this is impossible. You can do it if you play only one hand at a time and only one or two measures at a time. This step is important because fingering that works in a slow tempo may not work well when you play fast.

9. Play a few notes directly before and after the part you've just fingered. Does your fingering fit with them? If not, make the necessary changes.

10. Once you have a good fingering, write it in the music so that you will use it every time you play the piece. Write all numbers if the passage is complicated, for example in a contrapuntal texture like a Baroque piece. Otherwise, write in enough numbers to guide you. In scale and arpeggio passages, what usually helps the most is to write in numbers for the third and fourth fingers and the thumb.

Finger Slips

If you misfinger something during practice—you might run out of fingers, for example, or play one finger twice in a row—stop immediately. Figure out how it should be done and write finger numbers into the music. If they are already written in, circle or highlight them and drill immediately by playing ten times with the correct fingering.

Changing Fingers

If you have more than two repeated notes in a row, try changing fingers: 4–3–2, for example, instead of 3–3–3. This may seem unnecessarily complicated but there is a good reason for doing it. If repeated notes are slow, changing fingers helps you play legato and expressively. And if the notes are fast, changing fingers helps you play clearly at high speed.

Singing Fingers

Play one voice at a time while you sing the finger numbers out loud. Singing the numbers sets the pattern in your brain.

Finger Patterns

When fingering repetitive patterns, or sequences, first try using the same fingering on every pattern. If keyboard geography causes problems in certain patterns, change the fingering to fit.

For example, figure 5.3 shows two similar phrases from Bach's G Minor Minuet. Play the first phrase and use the same fingers (3–4) to begin each group. If you are comfortable using your thumb on B♭ in the second measure, you have your solution. If not, the middle group must start with 2–3.

Fig. 5.3. J.S. Bach, Minuet in G Minor.

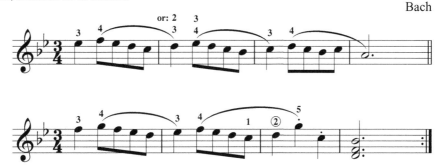

In the second phrase of figure 5.3, use the same fingering for each group, except for the D in the third measure. To accommodate the skip up to G, use 2 on D instead of 3.

ANOTHER KIND OF COMFORT: PEACE OF MIND

Playing the piano is complicated and requires intense concentration. But focusing too much on the complexity of the task can cause physical tension, and physical tension limits facility. So mental and emotional relaxation needs to be a part of practicing.

Every piece of music contains surprises, and surprises are always challenging. After a period of calm, there might be a flying leap or a sudden speed spurt. There might be an unexpected note or chord, a confusing cluster of notes, the first pedal mark in the piece, or some other abrupt change.

All these situations require fast action—mental or physical, or both. But don't expect to be able to react fast right from the beginning. You need time to consider what kind of shift is needed and how you are going to do it. If the composer doesn't give you that time—by means of a big rest, for example, or a *fermata*—take time yourself (and then give it back later) by doing the following tips. They will help you to be comfortable physically by allowing you to relax mentally.

Countdown
Draw a vertical line through the staff just before a sudden change, as in figure 5.4.

Fig. 5.4. J.S. Bach, Musette in D Major.

1. Starting several measures back, play up to your line and stop. Lift your wrists a bit so that your hands hover slightly above the keyboard with your fingers just barely grazing the key tops.

2. Count aloud slowly: "1, 2, 3, 4." If the next notes are far away, as in this example, float to the new position as you count.

3. Float back down to the keyboard, and play from the line to the end of the phrase.

4. Repeat three times, counting first to 3, then to 2 and then to 1.

5. Play the whole segment without counting and without stopping at the line.

This drill may solve your problem today, but not necessarily tomorrow. Like all practice tips, it needs to be done a number of times until you are so comfortable with a trouble spot that it no longer bothers you.

Mind Games
Pianists depend heavily on their eyes—carefully watching the music, the keyboard, their hands. Try using your eyes less. Rely instead on your sense of touch and hearing. This shift makes your mind work in a different way.

Play a portion of your piece while looking at the music. Now play it again, but this time close your eyes or look away—out the window, at the ceiling or at some object in the room. Even though your eyes are looking away, keep your ears and your brain focused on the music. Choose one aspect of your playing to think about, such as:

- Geography: which fingers play white and which play black keys? How many notes are there in a chord? Are there any skips? Any repeats?

- Phrase shape.

- Tone quality—of the melody, of the accompaniment.

- Balance between the hands.

- Pedal.

You don't have to memorize your piece before using this tip. You can do it any time: just keep the segment short.

Take Your Time
Sometimes playing a piece straight through from beginning to end causes a buildup of tension, even if you are only practicing and no one else is listening. Such anxiety can result in wrong notes or rhythms or even a loss of confidence.

If this happens, reduce the stress by pausing after each phrase and inserting an imaginary measure or two of rest. Use the rest to plan ahead. When you are ready, play the next phrase. Continue this way to the end of the piece.

Practice like this for several days or more. When you feel ready to put the piece back together, take out one rest, then two, then three, until you are again playing the piece without stopping from beginning to end.

CHAPTER 6
GETTING IT RIGHT

"I played it better at home!" Teachers hear this classic lament again and again. Have you ever said it? Were you amazed to hear yourself stumble in a certain spot? How could that happen—you played it perfectly at home.

Well, maybe… but maybe not. When you're at home, you probably play strictly for yourself. No one else is listening. In fact, you may not be listening closely yourself. The truth is that we all become less aware of mistakes when no one else is listening. We tolerate little stumbles. We say to ourselves, I'll fix that one later. Instead we often go on to other things and forget about the fixing.

Naturally, you want everything to be perfect at your lesson when you play for your teacher. Instead, to your horror, out pop those little errors. You may not even remember them from your practicing. All you know is that they sound horrible now. And you really believe that you played it better at home.

What probably happened, though, is that you made the same mistakes at home and just didn't notice. Learn to notice, because mistakes become habits, and habits are hard to break. If you correct mistakes the first time they happen, maybe you'll play it better at your *lesson*!

GENERAL ACCURACY DRILLS
The best way to prevent errors is to start smart (Chapter 1). Even if you do that, though, mistakes may still creep in. After practicing a piece for a while, your teacher may say, or you may discover from a recording, that you've learned some notes or rhythms wrong. Take action immediately. The drills in this chapter, if used faithfully every day, can solve the problem within a week.

Four First Steps
Play each section four times, but do something different each time. Use the following in any order.

- Sing the *count.*

- Sing the *note* names.

- Sing the *finger* numbers.

- Listen to the *dynamics.*

Baroque Song
If your piece is written in contrapuntal style, like a Bach invention, sinfonia or fugue, start out by using these steps:

1. Play each statement of the subject. Play it again, and this time sing along.

2. Play each countersubject twice, singing along the second time.

3. Play each subject while singing the countersubject, and then turn it around: play the countersubject while singing the subject.

FAD
Start a FAD—every day choose one piece, or one section of a piece, and check your *fingering, articulation,* and *dynamics.* Work on a different piece each day so that you cover all your pieces by the end of the week.

Sticker Spots
Take responsibility. If you make a mistake twice on the same note or rhythm, paste a small sticker or some removable highlighter tape about two measures before that spot. Whenever you see the marker, it will remind you of what's coming. This reminder may even keep you focused enough so that you avoid the mistake. Once you have played through the section many times without a problem (over a period of days or weeks), you can remove the sticker or tape.

You'll find that you will still be able to "see" the marker in your mind, even when you are playing from memory. This mental picture will remind you exactly where you are in the piece and what you need to watch out for.

Button Up
Here's a simple game to help deal with mistakes when they happen. Take six buttons (or pennies or candies) and arrange them in a row. As soon as you can play a tricky spot perfectly, move one button into a new row. Keep doing this until all the buttons have been moved to the new row. Repeat every day for one week.

Seven Up
Whenever you miss a note or rhythm or rest, stop and play it correctly seven times before you continue playing.

Troubleshooting
After you have practiced a piece a few times, you will find that some sections are harder than others. Assign a number to each trouble spot—#1 for the hardest, #2 for the next hardest, etc. Write these numbers in your score with a box or a circle around each number.

Whenever you practice the piece, begin with #1. Work on it as much as you can and then go on to #2, #3, etc. Once a section becomes easy for you, remove its number (and, if necessary, change the other numbers to fit). On the next day you'll have one less trouble spot to drill.

Do this every day until all the numbers disappear. It may take several weeks. If there is still a troublesome section, try memorizing it (Chapter 13). That will often solve the problem.

HIGHER MATH

When you encounter complicated rhythms, use one of the following tips immediately to unravel the mystery.

Math Counts

Occasionally you may look at a certain rhythm pattern and think, I have no idea how to count that. Use two tools to solve this problem—a pencil and a metronome.

1. Do the easy part first. Find some part of the measure or phrase where the counting is obvious. (Don't forget to include the first beat, the accompaniment, and the rests—they often provide important clues to solving a rhythm mystery.) For example, in figure 6.1, the obvious counts are the first counts of each measure, so write count 1 in both measures. Ignore the confusing rhythm of the melody and instead look at the accompaniment, which is much simpler. The first chord is a half note, so you can write count 3 over the note following the half note. And, since the note on count 3 is a quarter note, you can then write count 4 over the quarter rest. Now you already have almost all the counts written in.

Fig. 6.1. Haydn, Sonata, Hob. XVI/38.

2. Next determine where the missing counts go and write them in. In this example, you are looking for count 2. Here's the math part: you'll need to remember that one sixteenth-note triplet equals an eighth note and that four thirty-second notes also equal one eighth note. The dotted lines show where you would write either an "&" or the missing number 2.

3. Once you are sure your math is correct, set the metronome to one tick per sixteenth note. Leave out count 1 because of the triplets. Starting on count 2, clap or tap the rhythm of the melody with the metronome, counting aloud.

4. Play right hand alone from count 2 to the end with the metronome, still counting aloud. Repeat until it feels comfortable.

5. Now set the metronome tick to the eighth note and play again. This time, start from count 1. Remember to count aloud. Repeat until it feels easy. When you are ready, add the left hand.

Two-Against-Three Scale

Use a contrary motion C major scale to practice unmatching rhythms. In the following example, for two against three, play the right hand in triplets, three octaves up and down, while playing left hand in duplets, two octaves down and up.

Keep playing over and over. At first it will probably be uneven, but if you keep listening and playing you will begin to hear both parts better, and it will become more even. Play softly. It may help to make slight accents on the beats that your hands land on simultaneously. This technique sometimes works better if you close your eyes or at least look away from the keyboard. (Don't worry about the scale fingering—it will probably get mixed up, but that doesn't matter.)

Once you can do the scale with each rhythm sounding even, go back to your own piece and practice it in the same way.

Triplet Surprise

Sometimes when you are playing a piece made up mostly of quarter and eighth notes, you suddenly come across a triplet (fig. 6.2).

Fig. 6.2. Mozart, Minuet in F Major.

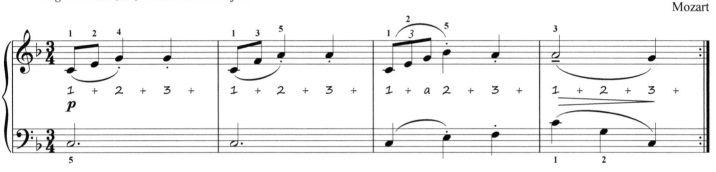

When that happens, stop and count aloud with the metronome, like this:

1. Set the metronome to tick on the quarter note. (If you set it to tick on each eighth-note, you'll have a problem in measure 3.)

2. Before playing, count aloud with the metronome:
   "1 & 2 & 3 &/ 1 & 2 & 3 &/ *1 & a* 2 & 3 &/ 1 & 2 & 3 &."

3. Make sure that your "*1 & a* 2 & 3 &" fits perfectly with the metronome ticks and that the "1 & a" counts are smooth and even.

4. Play, still counting aloud, still with the metronome, five times.

Common Denominator

Sometimes composers write unmatching rhythms, for example regular eighth notes in one hand against triplets in the other, as in the following example. You can count this rhythm by using common denominators. Multiply the number of regular eighth notes (two) by the number of triplets (three); this equals six. Each regular eighth gets three counts, each triplet eighth gets two counts.

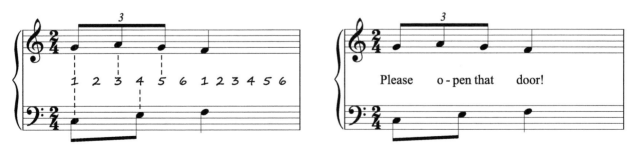

Start by playing and counting aloud very slowly. Gradually increase the speed until you can play the figure smoothly at the tempo you want. Or use words instead of numbers, like "Please open that door!"

CHORD CLUES

One reason so many people love the piano is that, unlike single-line instruments, it can produce harmonies. Anyone can play a chord or a tone cluster on a piano—we've all heard toddlers do it. Yet even accomplished pianists sometimes need special work on chord passages. After all, a single chord may contain 3, 4, 6, or even 10 notes, which is a lot to think about in itself. Add three or four different chords after the first one, and you have a real challenge. Give your brain a break by using the following tips to make chord patterns easier.

Chord ID

Many note errors result from too casual attention to chords. Take the time to get them right before you start.

1. Name each note of a chord from bottom to top and then from top to bottom.

2. Play the pitches one by one while naming them out loud, bottom to top, top to bottom.

3. Play the chord tones in different combinations, one note at a time. If your chord, for example, is DFA, play FA, FD, DA, AF, AD. Hum along, or better yet sing each note name as you play.

4. Play the chord tones in different blocks: solid thirds (FA, FD) and solid fifths (DA).

Countdown Chords

For a long series of chords, smooth the way from one chord to the next by playing the chords one by one, first four times each, then three times, then two times, and finally one time.

Chord Finger Tips

Fingering is a powerful tool. Writing in chord fingering can actually guide you to the right notes, because the finger numbers tell your hand how to space out the notes.

If you have room, write fingering next to chords instead of above them, so that it's easier to read at a glance.

In the example below, you can see immediately that the top and bottom notes are the same, and you know that you will use fingers 5 and 1 on those outer notes. With the help of the numbers 3 and 2, your hand will drop into the correct chord shape without your having to consciously think: That first chord has an A in the middle but the second one has a G. Once you get used to this system, you can take a shortcut by eliminating the 5 and 1 and just writing in the number for the middle note. If there are two notes in the middle, write numbers for both of them.

The more complex a chord is, the more writing in finger numbers will help you. To determine the best fingering, play blocked chords as broken chords, first from bottom to top, then from top to bottom. Always play them in context, that is, including the notes before and after. In his Prelude, Op. 28, No. 4 (fig. 6.3), for example, Chopin uses a series of constantly changing chords in the accompaniment. Taking the time to write in fingering for such passages before you even begin to practice them will always save you time in the long run.

Fig. 6.3. Chopin, Prelude, Op. 28, No. 4.

Chopin

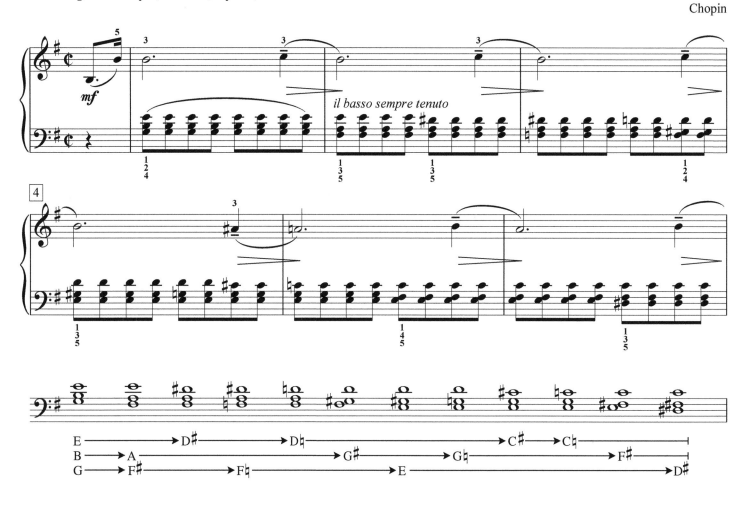

Common Tones

In a series of chords, the notes that stay the same from one chord to the next are called common tones. If you train yourself to recognize common tones, you'll find learning a chord series much easier.

Search for common tones before you begin practicing a chord series. Mark them in some way. You could draw a line connecting the common tones or, if they are whole notes, color code the noteheads so that you can see immediately which notes repeat and which notes change. The chord series in Chopin's Prelude No. 4 (fig. 6.3) is difficult to learn and, especially, to memorize, but understanding the common tone relationships will make the task much easier.

Slice & Dice Chords

Imagine that a series of three-note chords, instead of being simply clusters of notes on the piano, is a song sung by three people, each one singing his own part. For example, think of the chords in figure 6.4 as the voices of three singers—soprano (S), alto (A), and tenor (T).

1. Play each voice alone.

2. Play two voices together in every possible combination: ST, SA, AT.

3. Play all three voices together, as written, six times.

Fig. 6.4. Schumann, Kinderszenen, Op. 15, No. 6.

Add-a-Chord

This tip offers a slightly different drill for getting comfortable with a series of chords. It can be used on any number of chords. Here's how to apply it to a series of seven chords (fig. 6.5).

Fig. 6.5. Schumann, Kinderszenen, Op. 15, No. 6.

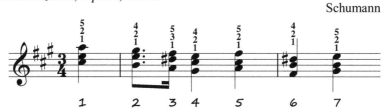

1. Write in all fingering and label each chord with a number.

2. Play chord #7 softly (but make sure you hear all notes) until it feels comfortable in your hand. Do the same thing with chord #6. Always use the fingering you've written in.

3. Play chords #6 and #7 back and forth slowly and softly until the movement feels natural and your fingers know where to go. Play the chords *without rhythm*, that is with all notes of an equal length. You can return the rhythm after you've mastered the chords.

4. When you feel as though you could play #6 and #7 on automatic pilot, move on to chords #5 and #6. When #5 and #6 are secure, play from #5 to the end five times. Move back to #4 and #5, then #3 and #4, then #2 and #3, and finally #1 and #2. Each time you perfect one pair of chords, attach them to the others by playing to the end of the chord series five times.

5. Play the whole chord row from beginning to end without the repetitions. Start slowly and softly, increase the speed as you like, and play the row enough times so that it feels easy. (Try this with your eyes closed.)

6. If you have removed a rhythm pattern, put it back in now and play the chord row several more times in correct rhythm. Check your fingering again.

INTRODUCING ORNAMENTS

At one time, pianists were accomplished at improvising ornaments on the spot. They would insert extra notes here and there to enhance the meaning of a phrase or just to make it sound more interesting.

Most pianists today lack this kind of training, so having to add ornaments to a piece can be a source of anxiety. There are actually a number of rules that can be learned and applied, and excellent guides to ornamentation can be found in music stores and online. Your teacher will guide you in the appropriate use of ornaments, and in time you can experiment with your own.

Practice each ornament by itself first. When you can play it comfortably up to tempo, add the accompaniment, then add the measures before and after it.

The most common ornament is a trill. The two components of a great trill are evenness and speed. Most pianists practice scales and arpeggios regularly, but seldom practice trills. Maybe that's why they dread trill passages. But anyone can develop good trill facility. Start with the *Trill Drill*, below. This exercise, if used on a daily basis, will increase speed and comfort on all types of ornaments.

Trill Drill

This is a hands-alone exercise, using the same set of fingering in each hand. You may trill on any keys you choose.

Always use the metronome on this drill so that your speed increases over time. Choose a comfortable speed to begin with, and set the metronome to a quarter note. At first your speed will rise steadily, but eventually you will reach a plateau: you may stay at the same speed for weeks or even months. This is normal. Keep doing the drill—you are still improving. Also, don't be surprised if your right hand can trill faster than your left hand. This is also normal.

The drill has three stages, each one more challenging. In each stage you will use all five fingers in trill combinations. Choose the stage that is best for you, or start with stage 1 and progress to stages 2 and 3 when you're ready. Use the given metronome speeds or change them to fit your needs, but start slowly enough to make the drill easy.

Stage 1. Turn the metronome on at 80 or slower. Before you start playing, count the rhythm out loud with the metronome a few times. Count "1, 2" on each tick for four ticks, and then say "hold" for four more ticks. Once your counting is steady, play the example with the metronome.

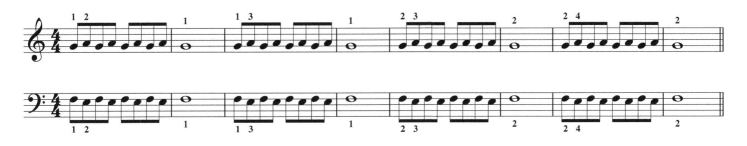

Stage 2. Turn the metronome on at 52 or slower. Before you start playing, count the rhythm out loud with the metronome a few times. Count "1, 2, 3, 4" on each tick for four ticks, and then say "hold" for four more ticks. Then change the rhythm: count "1, 2, 3" on each tick for four ticks, and then say "hold" for four more ticks. Once your counting is steady, play the following example with the metronome.

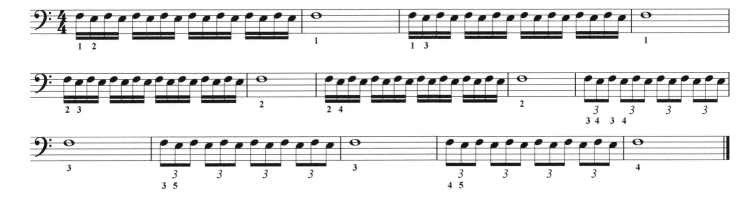

When you are comfortable with stage 2, remove all of the whole notes, going from one finger set to the other without pause.

Stage 3. Turn the metronome on at 40. Before you start playing, count the rhythm out loud with the metronome a few times. Count "1, 2, 3, 4, 5, 6, 7, 8" on each tick, and repeat four times. Then change the rhythm: count "1, 2, 3, 4, 5, 6" on each tick for four ticks. Once you can comfortably switch your counting from eight per tick to six per tick, you are ready to play. As shown below, trill eight notes to the tick with each finger combination: 12, 13, 23, and 24.

Without stopping, switch to six notes per tick and trill with the remaining finger combinations: 34, 35, and 45.

Ornaments by Ear

Sometimes the easiest way to learn an ornament is by ear.

Ask your teacher to play an ornament so that you can record it at your lesson. The ornament should be played several times—first alone and then with its accompaniment. Turn off the recorder and play the ornament yourself for your teacher, to make sure that you can do it correctly. Every day that you practice this piece, turn on the recorder and imitate your teacher's playing. Be sure that your teacher checks it at your next lesson, so that you know you have it right.

Paper Ornaments

If you take the time to write out an ornament, you will know it very well.

Consult your teacher, or a guide to ornamentation, to find out how an ornament should be played. Write the ornament out on a piece of manuscript paper, exactly as you plan to play it. (Use a pencil. You may have to erase a note or two before getting it right.)

1. Start with the clef signs and time signature.

2. Write in the ornament's notes.

3. Write in the counting, and check to be sure you have the right number of counts in the measure.

4. Write in the accompaniment. Align the notes carefully so that you can see which notes belong together.

Trill Fingers

Clever fingering can do wonders for ornaments.

Don't always use neighboring fingers on trills. Trilling with 31 or 42—especially when there's a black key involved—may keep the hand more relaxed and allow it to rotate, which can increase both speed and comfort.

When the upper note is a white key and the lower note is a black key a half step lower, as in the following example, try using 1 on the white key and 3 on the black key. This sounds backwards but is very comfortable.

Playing a turn or a mordent requires speedy repetition of one or two notes. Avoid using the same finger on the repeating notes: switching fingers enables you to play the ornament faster.

The following example shows a turn that includes three Cs. Instead of repeating the same finger three times, you can repeat it twice, or even avoid repeating it at all.

Similarly, a mordent's repeated notes will be cleaner (and can be played faster) if you use a little variety in the fingering.

Ornament Prep

If your hand is tight when you start an ornament, chances are that some of the notes will not sound. Using Bach's Invention No. 1 (fig. 6.6), try these steps to build relaxation into your ornament.

Fig. 6.6. J.S. Bach, Invention No. 1.

Bach

1. With one hand, play up to the ornament and pause.

2. Lift your hand a bit so that it hangs slightly above the keyboard with your fingers just barely grazing the key tops.

3. Play the ornament.

4. Repeat the first three steps several times, always giving your hand a chance to relax before playing the ornament.

5. Eliminate the pause, but try to keep the looseness you felt in your hand just before playing the ornament.

This exercise is especially useful for making sure that your ornament starts on the beat rather than before the beat. When you drop your hand into the ornament, make a little accent on the first note. This will help you to play it exactly with the left hand note.

CHAPTER 7
BUILDING FLUENCY

Some sections of a piece are easy to play from the beginning, some are difficult, some may even seem impossible. This chapter provides practice techniques that will help you unravel the mysteries and surmount the difficulties so that your piece will begin to take shape as a complete musical story.

The first practice tip, *Keep Track*, is used by all musicians—violinists, pianists, clarinetists, timpanists, old and young, professionals and students—though different people may call it by different names. The idea is simply to start at a comfortable pace and build up speed by playing slightly faster on every repetition.

Don't try to save time by doing this practice tip without a metronome. If you do, you will increase the speed too much too soon, causing mistakes. Then comes annoyance, frustration, and maybe even giving up. When you use a metronome, each notch up increases the speed in such small increments that you hardly feel or hear any difference. Even so, you know that you are improving because you see the numbers rising.

Keep Track

1. Play the problem passage through so slowly that you can play it perfectly. Stop playing and tap the beat. Turn on the metronome and find that speed.

2. Play the passage with the metronome one time, perfectly.

3. Raise the speed one notch (for example, from 60 to 63) and play again. (If you have a digital metronome, you can raise the speed by three or four numbers.)

4. Each time you play perfectly, raise the speed one notch. If you start to feel anxious or if you make a mistake, it's time to stop.

5. Write the day's best score in your music or in your assignment book or on a separate sheet of paper.

6. The next day, start over at step 2 at the previous day's final speed. Sometimes yesterday's speed will feel too fast. If it does, set the metronome back a notch or two and start from there instead.

A week's scores might look like this:

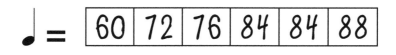

Notice that your speed doesn't always increase from one day to the next. That is all right, and it does not mean that you won't be able to raise the speed the next day. Increases are usually greater at the beginning of the week and smaller as the days go by.

Doing this drill a few times is not enough, even if you reach the correct tempo for the piece. To have a lasting effect, it should be repeated daily until the passage is thoroughly comfortable at or even above the desired tempo. This process could take days or, with an advanced piece, even weeks.

Opposites Attract

Play around with opposites when you are learning a piece. Surprisingly, playing something differently from the way it's written can actually improve your skill on the original material. Doing something "wrong" makes you realize, and remember, what is "right." (And it's fun to experiment like this.) For example:

- If the passage is legato, play it staccato and vice versa.

- If the passage consists of broken chords, play them blocked and vice versa.

- If the dynamic mark is *forte*, play *piano* and vice versa.

- If the tempo is *allegro*, play *adagio* and vice versa.

Caterpillars

1. When you can play one section of your piece perfectly, repeat it five times.

2. Do the same with the next section.

3. Hook the two sections together and play them five times in a row.

4. Keep using this formula until you have covered the whole piece.

Get Together

Once a passage feels good hands alone, you will want to hear how it sounds hands together. But keep in mind that playing hands together is at least twice as difficult as playing hands alone. It makes no sense, therefore, to try hands together at the same speed as hands alone (although this is what people usually do). Instead, try the following:

1. Turn on the metronome and find a comfortable hands-separate speed.

2. Decide which hand is more difficult. Let's say it's the right hand. Then its best speed will be slower than the left hand's. Cut the slower speed in half. (Either move the metronome down from, say, 100 per quarter to 50 per quarter, or keep the same metronome speed but change the meaning of each tick. For example, if your speed is 100 per quarter, keep the metronome at 100 but make each tick equal an eighth note instead of a quarter.)

3. Play hands together at this speed: it should be perfect. It may seem extreme to cut the speed back this much, but doing so almost always results in success on the first try. If you still have difficulty, find a slower speed that works for you.

4. Finish by doing **Keep Track** hands together.

Baby Steps

Nearly every piece contains some passages that become stumbling blocks. They need to be repeated perfectly many times in order to become easy. In a passage containing only white notes, make the repeats more interesting by doing them on different keys. Figure 7.1 shows how to do this on a tricky measure of Burgmüller's *Avalanche*.

Fig. 7.1. Burgmüller, Avalanche, Op. 100, No. 15.

Burgmüller

etc. up to C

1. Play the passage slowly enough to get it exactly right.

2. Move to the next key up or down and play it there.

3. Keep going until you have played the passage from every white key in the octave. Be sure to use the same fingering each time.

4. You may keep the speed constant or you may increase it, as long as you remain comfortable.

Giant Steps

To perfect a short passage that contains both black and white notes, do your repetitions like this:

1. Play the passage slowly enough to get it exactly right.

2. Move one octave up or down and play it there.

3. Keep going until you have played the passage in every octave of the piano. Use the same fingering each time.

4. You may keep the speed constant or you may increase it, as long as you remain comfortable.

You can use this to drill either one hand at a time or two hands together.

An alternative approach is to put a giant step *between* your hands. If your piece calls for playing one octave apart, for example, play two octaves apart or even three or more. When you separate your hands, the passage will not only feel different but it will sound different. You may discover things about it that you haven't heard before. And when you go back to your normal one-octave-apart mode, it will seem easier to play than it did before.

Combinations

When both hands are playing in parallel motion (fig. 7.2), it can be difficult to keep the hands exactly together. To address this problem, play hands together, staccato and *piano* in one hand, legato and *forte* in the other. Reverse.

Fig. 7.2. Hässler, Minuetto.

Mixed Media

This drill is the piano player's equivalent of a tongue twister.

Play both hands, but with only one hand on the keys. "Play" the other hand on the ledge above the keyboard, on your lap, on your knee, on your piano bench. Reverse the hands. Finally, play both hands on the keyboard. It should seem easier than before.

Leave Me Alone

It's great to be able to play hands together, but don't abandon hands-separate practicing. If you continue practicing the difficult spots one hand at a time you will reach the stage of polishing your piece much sooner.

Mr. Alberti

There once was a composer named Domenico Alberti, who often wrote accompaniments that look like figure 7.3, left hand. Other composers tried it as well, but his name stuck to it: it came to be called an Alberti bass.

Fig. 7.3. Kuhlau, Scotch Dance No. 1.

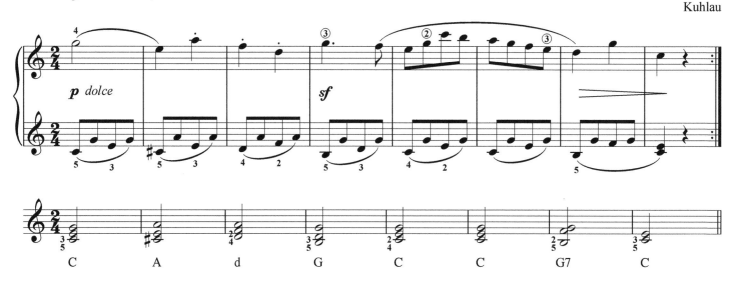

Even though this kind of accompaniment is just a broken chord, it is not as easy as it looks. Usually it must be played much faster than the melody notes, and it's almost always played by the weaker hand, the left hand. So practice an Alberti bass by itself, even if you find it less interesting than the melody.

1. If you have not already done so, do **Chord ID** (Chapter 6) so that you know what chords you're working with.

2. Write in the fingering. (You won't need to write in the finger number of the note that repeats over and over.)

3. Change the broken chords into block chords and play the chord progression slowly—one chord per harmonic change. If you have difficulty playing the progression smoothly, use **Countdown Chords** or **Add-a-Chord** (both Chapter 6) to get the notes into your fingers.

4. Playing the Alberti bass as written, use **Keep Track**, above, and work up to a tempo *higher* than your goal. You need this extra facility in order to be able to play the Alberti bass comfortably, no matter what the other hand is doing at the same time.

Spot Memory

Sometimes it's easier to play without the music than with it. For example, when you play large leaps with the music you must…

> look up at the page to read the notes,
> look down at the keyboard to see where your hands go,
> move your hands there to play,
> look up at the page again,
> and so on, back and forth. It's easy to get lost along the way and hard to play smoothly.

Another good spot to memorize early is one that is full of accidentals, especially if it contains both sharps and flats. All those marks in the music make it look confusing and even forbidding. Memorize the spot so you can look at the keyboard instead of at the music.

So don't save memorizing just for performance. Whenever you find part of a piece tiring or frustrating or you worry that you can never master it, stop and memorize it. It may be only a few measures long, and you may be far from memorizing the whole piece. But once you eliminate the up and down eye motion, you'll find that it is suddenly much easier to play.

CHAPTER 8
PUTTING MEANING IN MUSIC

What turns notes into music? What makes music meaningful? The answer to both these questions lies in the way you treat each note, how you relate one note to another and what happens in between. Musical expression comes from timing, tone quality, and different levels and qualities of sound. With these tools you can shape a phrase, balance different elements, and highlight special moments.

This chapter gives tips and techniques for converting sound and silence into music.

DYNAMICS

In the early stages of practicing a piece, you may be concentrating mostly on mechanical issues, trying to get everything into your fingers and planning to add the dynamics later. It's fine to do some practice drills without expression, but be careful not to play that way too long, because the piece may become frozen in your imagination without dynamics. If you hear a piece often enough without any dynamics, you may end up playing it well mechanically but without musical meaning.

Dynamic means alive, energetic, electric. A composer inserts dynamic markings to show how we can give life to the music. Use the following practice tips to help you notice and fulfill the composer's intentions.

Express Train

Circle or highlight each dynamic mark in your piece. Start two measures before the first circle and continue playing two measures beyond it. Can you hear the change? If not, try again. Do the same thing for each dynamic mark you have circled.

Dynamic Journey

Take a trip through your piece's dynamic markings.

- Find all the *pianissimo* sections, and play them in a row.

- If your piece contains both *mezzo forte* and *forte* sections, play them all—first a *mezzo forte* section and then a *forte* section. Can you hear the difference?

- Compare *forte* sections to *fortissimo* sections.

- Find the loudest and the softest spots in your piece. Label each spot with a sticker or some other special marker that will catch your eye.

Calm Down

Most pianists are very good at *crescendos*, but not so good at *decrescendos* (*diminuendos*). Go through your piece and put a dynamic mark at the beginning and end of every *diminuendo*. Play and listen to each one: did you follow the marks faithfully?

Terraced Dynamics

Instead of a gradual increase or decrease in volume (*crescendo* or *decrescendo*), you can make a sudden change from one dynamic level to another. This is called terraced dynamics. It was common in the Baroque period, but can be used in any style. One good use of terraced dynamics is to highlight sequences.

Figure 8.1 is a passage from Schumann's *Album for the Young*. The dynamic mark for the piece is simply *piano*. That does not mean that Schumann intended every note to be played *piano*. Try the passage with terraced dynamics—*piano, mezzo piano*, and *mezzo forte*. This is the kind of subtle change that composers often leave up to the performer. You can probably find sequences in your piece that would sound good with terraced dynamics.

Fig. 8.1. Schumann, Album for the Young, Op. 68, No. 1.

Sigh Search

Two-note slurs have a special meaning. In the Baroque period, they were played in a highly expressive way, with the second sound so soft that the two sounds together seemed like a sigh. Usually the first note was dissonant to the harmony, and the second note provided the resolution. Playing louder on the dissonance added spice to the music, and playing softer on the consonance made the resolution even sweeter. We still honor this tradition and enjoy this effect.

Composers do not normally write in dynamics on two-note slurs. They expect us to know what to do. To help you remember, find every two-note slur in your piece and write a small *decrescendo* sign over or under it. When you play these slurs, make the *diminuendo* extreme. You can also think, "loud/soft," "drop/roll," "down/up," "fall/rise," or "deep/shallow"—whatever image works best for you.

THE SOUND OF SILENCE

Actors, comedians, and good storytellers employ silence for dramatic effect. Silence is important in music, too. Composers use silence to make sound more meaningful. They may even exaggerate the dramatic effect of silence by placing fermatas over rests (fig. 8.2):

Fig. 8.2. Chopin Nocturne, Op. 32, No. 1.

Beethoven, in the famous motif from his Fifth Symphony (fig. 8.3), magnifies the power of the sounds by separating them with silence.

Fig. 8.3. Beethoven, Fifth Symphony.

Beethoven

Pianists tend to ignore rests or forget about them or use them literally to rest in the keys, which of course creates sound rather than silence—just the opposite effect from the composer's intentions. Since silence adds so much meaning to sound, observing rests is an indispensable habit to acquire. Some rests make music more intense, some rests relax it. Some rests are funny, some rests build suspense. A rest can strengthen rhythm or destroy it. Here are several ways to make rests work for you.

Rest Rhythm

Make your silences just as strongly rhythmic as your sounds. Check your rest rhythm by counting aloud. Lift at exactly the instant you say the count, not before and not after.

Or, try purposely eliminating rests and consider how that changes the effect. For example, play the excerpt from Bach's March in D (fig. 8.4), but ignore the rests completely. Next, play it again being very exact about the rests. Listen to the strong rhythmic impulse your silences create and how different the third measure sounds because it has no rests. Try this in your own piece.

Fig. 8.4. J.S. Bach, March in D.

Bach

Rest Message

Composers write rests for a reason, but it may not be the same reason from one rest to the next. We know that a rest means silence, but what kind of silence? Try to imagine what the composer intended each rest to mean, and show that in the kind of silence you create when you play.

Here are some possibilities:

    surprise
    suspense
    humor
    drama
    intensity
    peace
    rhythmic emphasis

As you decide what each silence in your piece means, write a little note in the music as a reminder.

Recognizing and Shaping Phrases

A phrase is a small amount of music, usually four measures, that makes sense when played alone. Think of it as a musical sentence. Composers often write phrases in groups (fig. 8.5). One phrase may sound like a question and the next like an answer. Or you might find four phrases that go together like a paragraph. They end with a strong cadence, and you sense that a new section is coming.

When we speak, our voices create a kind of song, rising or falling, speeding up or slowing down. Such changes in loudness, pitch, rhythm, and speed help us to express an idea or emotion so that people better understand our words.

The same thing is true of music. Composers give us guidance: they write the pitches and the rhythm, and sometimes they indicate loudness and speed. Even with all these instructions, though, something else must be added to make the music come alive. It's called shaping a phrase, or phrasing.

Since we humans speak from an early age, imitating the sounds we hear around us, nobody needs to tell us how to "shape" a sentence—we know how to express ourselves. Shaping a musical phrase isn't quite that easy. It requires some planning. We need to do it, however, because music loses its magic when all sounds are equal.

The best way to start is with the voice—speaking or, even better, singing. Without even thinking about it, we shape a song, usually by singing a little louder as the melody rises, softer as it descends, stressing important words and perhaps taking extra time at dramatic moments. Use these natural abilities to build beautiful musical phrases at the piano.

Phrase Shapes

A phrase of music, just like a phrase of words, only makes sense when it has a shape. We give it shape through the use of dynamics.

1. Pick out the melody of one phrase and play it without any accompaniment.

2. Play it again but this time sing along with it.

3. Sing the melody without playing. Listen to the shapes your voice makes—higher, lower, louder, softer.

4. Play the melody again without singing. Shape it the way you sang it. If you like the way it sounds, write dynamics in the score to help you remember this shape every time you play the melody.

If you have trouble singing the melody, or if your song does not sound like something you want to imitate, play the melody without singing.

1. Play it three times, changing the dynamics in some way each time.

2. Add the accompaniment and see how it fits in.

3. Choose the version that sounds best to you and write in those dynamics. Use pencil, in case you change your mind later.

Whatever shape you choose for your phrase, show that the phrase is finished by playing the final note softly (unless the composer puts an accent there). This creates a graceful ending to the phrase.

Phrase ID

Count the phrases in your piece. Mark each one with a long slur. Decide which phrase to practice, or do them all, but work on one at a time.

It's not always easy to identify phrases. Remember that although there is no rule about how many measures a phrase contains, the most common phrase length by far is four measures. So look for that first. Another clue may be the appearance of a long note or a rest at the end of several measures, as in figure 8.5.

Fig. 8.5. Beethoven, Russian Folk Song.

RUSSIAN FOLK SONG

Beethoven

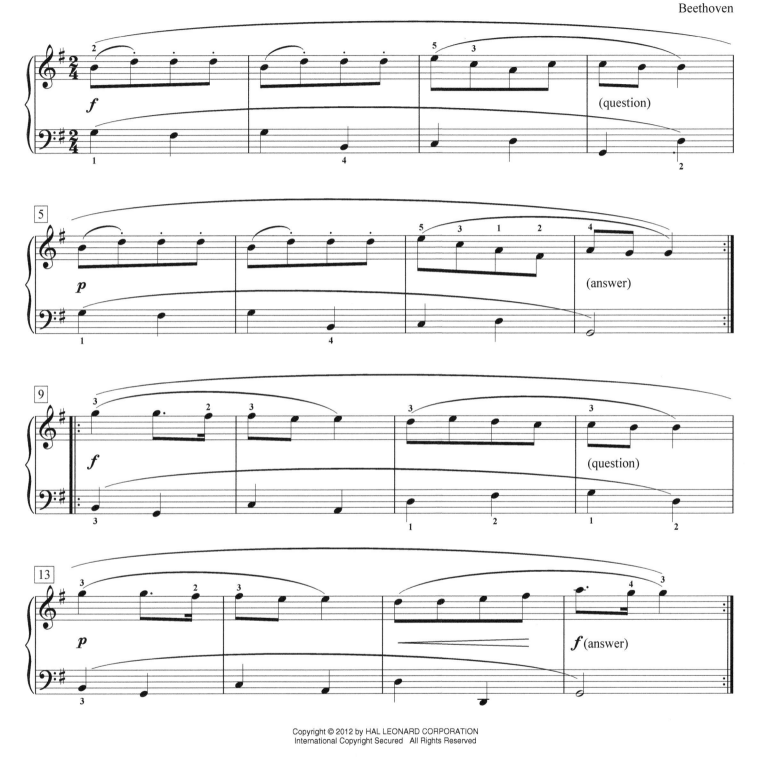

Over the Line

Music moves forward. Melodies move over bar lines. When you are identifying phrases, or practicing one phrase or even one motif at a time, don't stop at the bar line. Instead, go over the line to a point where the music makes sense. For example, in figure 8.6:

1. Play the melody, but stop at each bar line. How does it sound?

2. Play the same melody. This time, stop after the first note in each measure.

3. Play the same melody. Stop only when it sounds like a complete phrase.

Fig. 8.6. Turk, March in G Major.

MARCH IN G MAJOR

Turk

Punctuation Points

A cadence is a point of rest in music, caused by a succession of chords that creates a kind of punctuation in the music. Some cadences, for example, sound like commas or semicolons, others sound like periods, the end of a paragraph, or the end of the entire story.

How many cadences can you find in your piece? Mark each one. If you know the formal name (authentic, half or incomplete, plagal, deceptive), you can write that in. If you don't know these names, just write in what the cadence sounds like to you—comma, semi-colon, period, or paragraph.

Chord Talk

Harmony gives color and meaning to melody. Chords talk!

Play an accompaniment by itself in slow block chords. Listen: does one chord sound surprising or more interesting, more dissonant, or more beautiful than the others?

Play the phrase again, and this time emphasize the special chord. You can do this by

- making a *crescendo* to the chord and a *decrescendo* after it.

- inserting a tiny pause before playing the chord (agogic accent).

- accenting the chord.

- playing it suddenly softer (to be really different).

How does the melody interact with the harmony? You may find that the high point of the melody coincides with that special chord. Play the melody and accompaniment together, and exaggerate the shape that you've chosen.

ADDING PEDAL

The piano is by its nature a percussion instrument. It can make sharp, short sounds. It can also make fairly long sounds—the better a piano's quality, the longer a single sound lasts. (Hold down one key on your piano and count how many seconds the sound lasts.) The nature and length of a piano's sound can be altered through the use of pedals. These are wonderful tools. When used properly, they can make us forget we are playing a "percussion" instrument. Pedals give the piano greater expressive range and allow it to become a singing instrument.

Most grand pianos have three pedals. Upright pianos usually have two, but some have a middle pedal that causes a felt cloth to drop between the hammers and the strings, which drastically mutes the sound.

Soft Pedal

The pedal on the left is the soft pedal, or *una corda* pedal. On a grand piano it shifts the whole action slightly to the right—you can actually see the keyboard move. Now the hammers that normally strike three strings will strike only two, which decreases the volume.

The soft pedal also affects tone quality to a greater or lesser extent, depending on the piano. To understand why, examine the felts on your piano hammers. Unless the instrument is brand new, you will see three grooves in the felt, caused by the three strings that the hammer usually hits. When the action is shifted by the soft pedal, the hammer strikes the string on ungrooved felt, which dulls the sound. This change in tone quality is similar to the use of a mute on a string instrument. It will diminish a tone's singing quality, but on the other hand its mysterious, veiled quality can provide magical contrasts.

The sign for using the soft pedal is "U.C.," which stands for *una corda*—in English, one string. When this term was first used, each piano key had only two strings, and the soft pedal shifted the action so that only one string was struck. Today most keys have three strings. Thus the sign to remove the soft pedal is *tre corde*, or three strings.

On an upright piano the soft pedal moves the hammers closer to the strings, reducing the distance and speed of the hammers' strikes. The volume is reduced but the basic tone quality remains the same.

Damper Pedal

The pedal on the right is the damper pedal. This is the one that we use the most; it's usually referred to simply as "the pedal." If someone says, "Use pedal in this measure," they mean use the damper pedal.

To see how this pedal works on a grand piano, open the lid and remove the music desk. Press the damper pedal. You will see the whole bank of dampers lift away from the strings. If you sing or shout into the piano with the pedal down, you will discover how much the piano's strings respond, even when nothing but sound waves are striking them.

Using the damper pedal can blend sounds together to make a mysterious, foggy, or watery sound. Play this, for example, with the damper pedal depressed from beginning to end:

Because of sympathetic vibrations, the damper pedal can also enlarge and extend a sound, such as a big ending chord.

Experienced pianists often use the pedal to make a piano's sound more beautiful, more singing, less percussive. But the most common use of the pedal is to connect sounds without blurring them together. This technique is called syncopated, or legato, pedal (see *Pedal Counts*, below).

Postpone using the pedal on a new piece until you have learned to connect melody notes with your fingers, that is, to play legato. When it's time to add pedal, do it deliberately: follow either the pedal marks in the piece or your teacher's instructions.

Pedal Counts

To connect one note to another with the damper pedal, you must learn legato pedaling. This type of pedaling is not as simple as plopping the foot down and lifting it up every once in a while. It requires good coordination and alert ears, and it takes time to perfect.

The eight bars below are an exercise for legato pedaling. (Playing these chords will give you a rich sound, but you can create an easier exercise by using single notes instead of chords.)

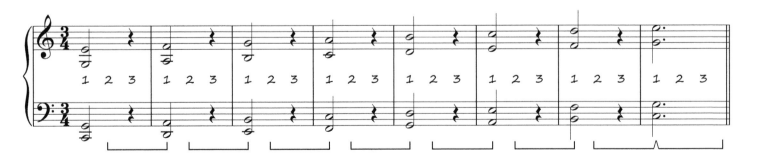

Set the metronome to a slow speed (50 to 60 to the quarter). Count one or two measures aloud with the metronome before starting to play. Then:

1. Play on "1."

2. Put the pedal down on "2."

3. Lift your hands—but not your foot!—and move to the next position on "3."

4. On count "1", play the next chord and at the same instant lift the pedal.

5. Repeat steps 2 to 4 on measures 2–7.

6. On the last measure, lift the pedal on "1" as usual, but put it down again right away and hold it to the end of the measure.

Notice that you kept the pedal *down* while moving to a new harmony and that you kept it down until you played the new chord. If you lift the pedal early, the two chords will not be connected. Also, if you lift the pedal too early you are likely to put it down again too soon, which will blur the old sound into the new sound. When your pedal timing is perfect, you will hear two harmonies, smoothly connected but distinct from one another.

Once you can do this exercise easily, adapt it to the pedaled portions of your piece. Alter the counting to fit the piece.

Pedal Plus

When first adding pedal or when you need to clean up your pedaling, practice each pedaled passage as follows:

1. pedal + left hand

2. pedal + right hand

3. pedal + hands together

This sequence allows your ear to hear one layer of pedaled sound at a time, the better to help your foot pedal cleanly.

Sostenuto Pedal

The middle pedal—the pedal that may be missing on an upright—is called the sostenuto pedal. To see how it works on a grand, open the piano lid and remove the music desk. Strike a key, let's say low D, at the same time that you depress the sostenuto pedal. You will see D's damper rise. Continue holding the sostenuto pedal down and play some other keys. Their dampers will remain down, thus allowing you to sustain the D as if you were using the damper pedal, while playing other notes as if you were not using the damper pedal. (You can even play them staccato and still hear the long tone underneath.) In theory the sostenuto pedal is a great tool, especially for virtuoso Romantic and Contemporary literature. In practice, however, it is tricky. It is not as easy to engage the sostenuto as it is to use the other pedals, and it works slightly differently on every piano. This presents a problem for someone who is practicing on one piano but planning to perform on another.

PART III POLISHING A PIECE

Once basic structure, notes, rhythm, and dynamics have been learned, you can start to polish your piece, bring it up to speed, and find solutions through the practice tips for any technical challenges that remain.

Chapter 9 offers additional ideas for maintaining comfort during the polishing process.

Chapter 10 helps you clear up any remaining accuracy issues.

At this point you will be spending a fair amount of time working your piece up to tempo. Chapter 11 gives you new ideas on how to do that efficiently.

Chapter 12 returns to the issue of expression and provides tips on dynamics, phrasing, and pedaling.

Stay on task by reviewing three key practice tips. If you still have numbered trouble spots, apply **Troubleshooting** (Chapter 6) to continue drilling them until all the numbers have been erased. If, nevertheless, a section that bothers you remains, try memorizing it. That will often solve the problem.

Continue to use **Back Up** (Chapter 4) on any troublesome passage. At this stage you might also use **Back Up** to build overall continuity. Divide your piece into large sections and put the sections together back to front until you can play the entire piece up to tempo without any stops or mistakes.

Finally, apply **FAD** (Chapter 6) as you did in the early stages of practicing.

- Check your *fingering* whenever you stumble. Are you really following the fingering you intended to use? If not, return to the correct fingering and drill until it feels solid. If you are following the planned fingering but still stumbling, consider finding a new fingering.

- Check your *articulation* by recording yourself. In the recording can you hear the difference between staccato and legato? Is every accent clear?

- Check your *dynamics* by recording yourself. Listen to the recording while following the score to be sure that every dynamic indication is being observed. Or ask a practice partner to listen and tell you each time the level of dynamics changes. Compare that reaction to the marks in the score.

CHAPTER 9
PLAYING WITH COMFORT

By now you should be comfortable with most of your piece. Devote the bulk of your time and energy to the parts that still feel difficult. Reward yourself for a good practice session by playing through the parts that have become easy.

No matter how carefully you worked on fingering in the early stages of practicing, problems may still arise during the polishing process. Problems could be due to a new tempo or to a sudden difficulty coordinating the hands or even to a change in dynamics.

It is all right to revise fingering if necessary. Obviously, you should avoid redoing it too often, because you want the habits you form to be lasting ones and to help you reach the automatic pilot stage. But if you need a change, go back to the **10-Step Finger Guide** (Chapter 5) and find a new solution. Don't forget to write the new fingering in the music.

Pay close attention to your physical comfort at the piano as you polish your piece (review **Good Moves** and **Starting Lineup** in Chapter 5). If you experience any kind of pain while practicing, stop playing and tell your teacher immediately.

Countdown (Chapter 5) is helpful at all stages of practicing. You can either use it in the standard way, by actually counting down during rest stops, or you can adapt it by simply inserting a slight pause in the flow before a difficult spot and then repeating the process until you can remove the pause and continue playing without a bump.

As you increase your speed in polishing a piece, coordination problems may arise. Use the following tips to regain comfort.

High Fives

Use large muscle movement to solve coordination problems. Start big because it's easier that way. When you feel more comfortable, move less.

Figure 9.1 shows a phrase where each hand alternates between legato and staccato—already a challenge—and in addition the parts are staggered so that one hand has to play staccato while the other hand plays legato.

Fig. 9.1. Tchaikovsky, Waltz, Op. 39, No. 8.

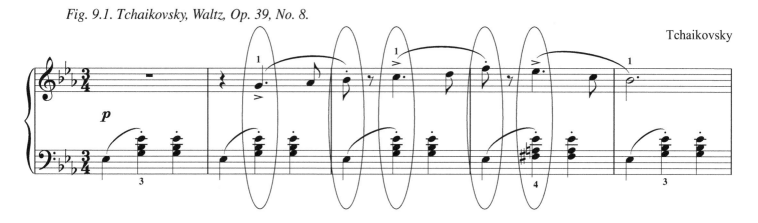

Try the following on this example. Then you can adapt it to your own piece.

1. Circle each trouble spot. Tap the left-hand rhythm. Count aloud as you tap. When you tap legato notes, keep your hand close to the table surface. When you tap staccato notes, use the table like a springboard—float your arm and hand a foot or two up into the air.

2. Repeat with the right-hand rhythm.

3. Tap the rhythm hands together, counting aloud. Use the exact same movements that you made in steps 1 and 2.

4. Do steps 1 and 2 again, this time playing the notes hands alone. Use your tapping movements as a model: stay close to the keys on legato notes; spring into the air from the staccato notes (you are using large muscle movements). Repeat five times.

5. Hands together, very slowly, play each circled spot by itself. Use the same exaggerated lift on each staccato note, and hold the legato note long enough to hear it sound alone. Repeat five times.

6. Add the remaining notes (hands together). Keep using exaggerated movements until you can play the example smoothly and all articulation is perfect. Then reduce the movements to a minimum—by now you should be comfortable with small muscle movement.

Playing Around

This tip is fun. It gives you something different to listen to and makes repetitions more interesting. It's a good way to practice a short trouble spot in one hand—one measure or even less, as in figure 9.2.

Fig. 9.2. Chopin, Waltz, Op. 69, No. 2.

1. Write in a finger number for every note. Make sure that this is the fingering that you ultimately want to use and that it fits the measure before and the measure after.

2. Play the passage slowly, softly, and perfectly, three or four times. And then play it backwards.

3. Now play around with it. Go up and down without a stop, as many times as you want, in a kind of circle. It's all right to speed up as long as you don't stumble.

4. When you have finished playing around, play the passage in its original form, connecting it to the measures before and after. It should feel easier than it did before.

Left Aid

Most pianists, even naturally left-handed pianists, have less facility in the left hand than in the right, probably because the right hand almost always has more to do, so it gets more practice. As a result, fast passages in the bass clef often cause problems. When they do, follow these three steps.

1. Practice the left hand by itself until it feels and sounds good. Use ***Stop-and-Go***, ***Finger Gym***, or ***Regroup*** (all in Chapter 11) to strengthen the fingers.

2. Play hands together five times, *forte* in the left hand and *pianissimo* in the right.

3. Play hands together three times with normal dynamics.

CHAPTER 10
STAYING ON TRACK

You are in the final stages of polishing a piece. It's time to double-check all the mechanical details. This chapter introduces additional practice tips for maintaining accuracy and clarity, locking in patterns of rhythm and pulse, and polishing ornaments.

NOTE ACCURACY AND CLARITY

Now that your speed is increasing, it is important to keep listening for clarity. Can you hear every note you play? If some are missing or sound blurry, bring them back into focus with the following practice tips.

If you have any difficulty remembering a chord sequence or playing every chord tone clearly, return to ***Slice & Dice Chords*** (Chapter 6) to refresh your memory of the keyboard geography involved.

Clean-Up Time

1. Go through your piece and remove the sticker from any sticker spot that no longer bothers you.

2. If some stickers remain—spots that are still a problem—remove the markers and replace them with different markers. It could be a different color, larger writing, or a new sticker, but use something that is sure to catch your eye.

3. Play from four measures before each sticker spot to four measures after it, six times perfectly—no errors, no stumbles, no pauses.

4. Do this every day for a week.

5. The next week, play the piece through every day and keep track of errors.

6. At the end of the week, remove stickers from all the spots you have mastered.

Popcorn

As you play, imagine your fingers bursting out of the keys like popcorn popping. The sound will not be staccato and it will not be legato. It will be the sound called *leggiero*. It feels good, it sounds good, and it's perfect for a scale passage—especially a soft one—in Clementi or Mozart. This technique is also useful when you need to clean up muddy-sounding passages.

Listening In

When your piece begins to feel polished, record yourself and listen to the replay.

- Watch your music as you listen, and mark anything that needs improvement.

- Ask yourself, "What happened? Why? Which practice tips would help?"

- Use your chosen practice tips on those spots for several days' practice.

When you feel the problems have been solved, record yourself again. There still may be some issues or some new ones may crop up. If so, repeat the process until you are satisfied.

Tap Dance

Play a passage of fast notes staccato, with highly energetic finger action. Pretend your finger tips are tap shoes, clicking out the rhythm on the keys.

Look Again

Practice *with* the music.

- Look carefully at each mark in the music—dynamics, tempo indications, articulation.

- Double check any notes or rhythms that you once played wrong.

- Reread any directions from your teacher, and play the relevant passage to make sure you are following those directions.

Final Four

It's easy to lose control of the final group in each measure of a long, fast passage. At high speed the last few notes of each measure may blur together or even disappear.

Build your awareness of final groups, and train your fingers to play cleanly by practicing the last group of notes in each measure:

- staccato, or

- with a *crescendo* into the next measure, or

- suddenly *forte*.

Figure 10.1 shows sixteenth notes in groups of four. If your groups are different, call this tip "Final Three" or "Final Six" and use it the same way.

Fig. 10.1. Czerny, Study in G Major.

RHYTHM DRILLS

Rhythm issues should be under control by this stage of practicing. If you are still having trouble with any rhythms, consider this your most important problem to solve.

Rhythm Test

Once learned, a rhythm lives deep inside you. If you learned it wrong, you feel it wrong. And that makes it difficult to change. You need help!

Use two practice partners—a metronome and either another person's ear or a recorder.

1. Set the metronome to the smallest note value so that you don't rush on long notes. Play with the metronome five times, counting aloud.

2. Turn off the metronome and play three more times, still counting aloud. Check with your practice partner to see if your rhythm was correct.

3. Play two times without the metronome and counting silently. If your rhythm is still correct, you are finished for the day.

4. Do this every day for a week.

Rest Check

Each day pick a different section of your piece to check for rests. First play only the measures that contain rests. Listen to each silence, and count how long it lasts. Then play the whole section, counting aloud. Make sure that you hear every silence and that each rest is mathematically correct.

Yellow Light

Slow down at a *ritardando*, but don't stop the music. In a *ritardando* the pulse is stretched, like a rubber band. If the *ritardando* is too extreme the music stops flowing, just as a rubber band breaks if stretched too far. Record your piece and listen to see if the *ritardandos* in your playing are yellow lights or red lights.

ORNAMENTS

Trills, mordents, turns, and all similar ornaments are added to the music as decorations. People who wear jewelry are careful to choose baubles that fit their clothes and their personalities. Do the same with musical ornaments. Ornaments should never overwhelm the notes they are decorating, so play them at the same level or softer than the principal notes. And always play an ornament in the same character as the music around it.

Trill Steps

It isn't always necessary to play a trill fast. Even if you intend it to be fast eventually, build the speed step-by-step.

Start out by matching the trill rhythm to the accompaniment, as in the example below. When that feels easy, increase the number of trill notes—using the same basic pulse—until you are satisfied with the speed and number of notes. If you still want it faster, you may play a free trill, that is, play it as fast as you like (as long as it stays even).

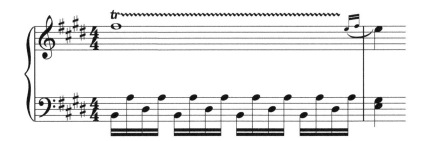

Ornamental Moods

Go through your piece and play each ornament, first by itself and then within its phrase. Think about the music's mood and tempo. Match the ornament to the music. In a fast movement, make it sound brilliant or funny or exciting. In a slow movement it should sing just as beautifully as the main melody notes sing.

Trills & Company

Pianists typically worry so much about playing trills that they stop listening to the trill's accompaniment, unaware that the accompaniment is sloppy or even incomplete. Not only does this sound messy, but if notes are rushed or left out of the accompaniment, the measure will be missing a half beat or even a whole count, which certainly upsets the pulse.

To fix this problem, practice a trill passage as shown below. Count the entire measure aloud, but don't start playing until the fourth beat. (If the composer has indicated a specific way to finish the trill, take care of that first.) Once you can do the fourth beat perfectly, start on the third, then the second and finally the first.

Record your playing, listen to the recording, and make sure you can hear every left hand note. If this doesn't solve the problem, reduce the speed of your trill to match the notes of the left hand (see *Trill Steps* on page 64).

CHAPTER 11
BUILDING SPEED

Working a piece up to speed occupies a major portion of practicing. Keep your work interesting and productive by using a variety of speed drills.

My teacher at Indiana University, Gyorgy Sebok, once listened to me struggle through a difficult passage, and asked, "How did you practice that?" I replied proudly, "I practiced it slowly." After a long pause, Mr. Sebok said quietly, "And do you plan to perform it slowly as well?"

Playing the piano, he went on, is like water skiing—it can't always be practiced slowly. Not that we can't ever prepare for speed by practicing slowly, but at a certain point we must adopt the gestures, and the reflexes, of playing fast.

Many practice tips in this chapter are about practicing fast, usually in small doses. A measure or a phrase is perfected and then combined with another and another. Practicing in this way is like doing a jigsaw puzzle, only more interesting and rewarding.

For building speed, *Keep Track* (Chapter 7) remains an effective practice tool. Your metronome marker scores will not rise as dramatically as they did in the early stages, though. A week's scores might look like this:

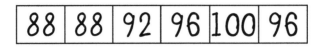

Even though your score stayed the same one day and actually went down another day, you still progressed from 88 to 96 in one week, and tomorrow you'll probably hit 100 again.

Every finger is a different size and shape—and then there is the thumb! No wonder it is so difficult to play a simple five-finger pattern perfectly evenly. And evenness must come before speed if we want the music to remain clear and brilliant. Tips in this chapter show ways of promoting finger independence so that speed doesn't spoil clarity. Other tips address the issue of keeping keyboard movements comfortable and economical, another necessity for building speed.

Finger Gym

To smooth out a rough spot or work up the speed of a difficult passage, use different accent patterns so that you train all fingers equally. Every time you change the pattern, you are putting different fingers in the spotlight. This drill increases finger independence and leads to more even, fluent playing.

Since this is a finger exercise and since your goal is to play fast, make all accents with your fingers, not with your wrist and never with your forearm or whole arm.

1. Play through a passage accenting the first note of each group of notes—for example the first of four sixteenths.

2. Play again, this time accenting each group's second note.

3. Repeat, accenting the third note and finally the fourth note.

4. Finish by playing the passage as many times as you like with no accents at all.

Fast notes are usually beamed together in groups of three, four, or six. The measures below show how to do *Finger Gym* when each group contains four notes, but you can adapt it to groups of three or six.

Stop-and-Go

This practice tip makes a long, hard passage feel and sound different. It improves finger independence because each rhythm you use challenges different fingers. This drill not only helps you master the passage, it strengthens your overall technical facility.

Do it while looking at the music, even if you know your piece from memory. You may need to write in additional fingering, because you'll be stopping and starting at unaccustomed places.

Pick a rhythm pattern, below, and apply it to the entire passage that you want to improve. The ● indicates a short note, and the ▬ indicates a long note.

Use rhythms 1 to 6 in a passage with notes grouped in fours—four eighth notes, four sixteenths, four thirty-seconds.

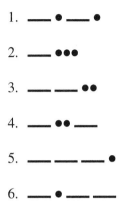

1. ▬ ● ▬ ●

2. ▬ ●●●

3. ▬ ▬ ●●

4. ▬ ●● ▬

5. ▬ ▬ ▬ ●

6. ▬ ● ▬ ▬

Use rhythms 7 to 10 in a passage with notes grouped in threes.

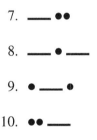

7. ▬ ●●

8. ▬ ● ▬

9. ● ▬ ●

10. ●● ▬

Use rhythms 11 to 16 in a passage with notes grouped in six.

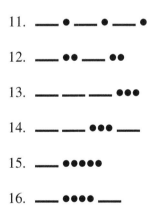

11. ▬ ● ▬ ● ▬ ●

12. ▬ ●● ▬ ●●

13. ▬ ▬ ▬ ●●●

14. ▬ ▬ ●●● ▬

15. ▬ ●●●●●

16. ▬ ●●●● ▬

Fast version. Play the short note or notes as fast as you can without blurring them. They should not sound like grace notes; they should be bright and clean, almost staccato. Shoot each finger up out of the key after it plays. After you whiz through the short notes, though, take time to relax and plan your next move. Think of every ▬ note as a fermata: sit on each one, relax your hand, and picture the notes and fingering of the next fast group before actually playing it.

Slow version. Play slowly and rhythmically with a strong, deep finger action. Lift each finger before dropping it into the key.

Broad Jumps

Typically a pianist plays more or less in the center of the keyboard or else moves gradually to the right or the left. But sometimes the music calls for big leaps. Even in a slow tempo a leap can be difficult. When the tempo is fast, it may seem impossible.

To make leaps possible and even comfortable, pretend you are an athlete doing the broad jump. Picture the distance you plan to cover, the way athletes do imaging. Name the interval and the notes of the leap you're about to make. Once you have the distance clearly fixed in your mind, follow these steps:

1. Do a glissando covering the same distance as the leap you're practicing. Notice that your arm carries your hand, not the other way around.

2. Return to the original position and do the leap three times without actually playing any notes. Use the same arm movement you used on the glissando. Travel in a wide arc close to the keys. If your fingers stay extended in playing position, your hand will be tense, so relax it by letting your fingers hang down as you travel. Travel fast and land smoothly, touching the keys lightly but with no sound.

3. Repeat, but this time travel fast, land smoothly, freeze, and then play the notes.

4. Go back and forth until you feel that your arm knows the way and can land on target and play accurately five times in a row.

Most people have better muscle memory than they think. You may be amazed to find that you can even do this practice tip with your eyes closed.

Split Octaves

Practice an octave passage, such as figure 11.1, playing only the fifth fingers, then only the thumbs, then as written. When you practice pinkies only, keep the thumb side of your hand relaxed—do not freeze it open in octave position. Do this left hand alone, and then hands together.

Fig. 11.1. Beethoven, Ecossaise in G.

Beethoven

Over the Top

If you can run ten miles, running one mile is easy.

- Take part of a difficult passage and make it even more challenging. For example, if an arpeggio or scale in your piece is one octave long, make it two or three octaves long, or even extend it to the whole keyboard. When you can do this, one octave will seem easy.

- Do **Keep Track** (Chapter 7) on a difficult passage until you can play it even faster than you plan to play the whole piece. If this is impossible hands together, do it one hand at a time. It will still help you to play the passage better.

Regroup

This practice tip is good for a long stretch of fast notes. It takes concentration, and it will make the passage you're playing feel completely different. Try it on figure 11.2 and then adapt it to your own piece.

- If the notes are grouped in fours, regroup them into threes (as in fig. 11.2) or sixes; if notes are grouped in threes, regroup them into fours or fives; if notes are grouped in sixes, regroup them into fours. Have plenty of finger numbers written in the score so that you don't change the fingering. Watch the music carefully to keep you on track.

- Whatever the grouping is, drop into the first note of each group with a slight accent. This will help you play the entire group in one gesture.

- Practice a passage with the notes regrouped and then go back to the normal groupings. You will be surprised at how much more comfortable it is. You can almost feel your brain relaxing!

Fig. 11.2. Czerny, Study in G Major.

Handfuls

Typically, we think of notes in groups of four, six, or eight. For a change, group the notes according to fingering (fig. 11.3). This will increase your awareness of fingering patterns and hand movements.

Fig. 11.3. Clarke, March in D Major.

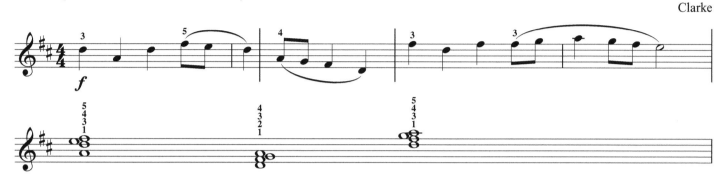

See how many notes you can play without moving your hand (if necessary, fill in some finger numbers to find the answer). Consider this group of notes as one handful.

1. Draw a line at the end of each handful.

2. Play the first handful as a block chord or a cluster. Repeat softly a few times so that your fingers get used to the feel of these keys under your hand.

3. Repeat step 2 with each handful.

4. Play each handful in single notes as written, softly and as many times as you like. Pause between handfuls, and take your time moving to the next position. Continue to the end of the passage.

5. When each handful feels comfortable by itself, put them all back together again one by one. You can start anywhere you like—at the end, at the beginning, or in the middle.

CHAPTER 12
FINDING DEEPER MEANING

As you polish your piece, dynamics become increasingly important. Examine all the dynamic markings and think about what they mean in the context of the whole piece.

There is more to dynamics than simply following *piano*, *forte*, and *crescendo* signs. You also need to put various voices in proper balance and bring out melody notes in chords. This is a kind of vertical dynamics and is essential to conveying music's meaning. Several tips in this chapter help accomplish this.

Also covered are ways to refine phrasing and pedaling. With most mechanical difficulties under control, you can now devote more of your practice sessions to listening to the shape of each phrase, each section, and the entire piece. This is a good time to focus more on pedaling, keeping in mind that the pedal is one of the most effective expressive tools pianists have.

DYNAMICS ON AND OFF THE PAGE

By now you should be very familiar with the composer's markings. Review all dynamics and make sure you are following them. Enhance your playing with more expression and the addition of your own dynamic ideas.

Shading

1. Decide exactly how you want the final note of a *crescendo* or a *decrescendo* to sound. Play the final note at that level.

2. Add the preceding notes, one at a time, shading them carefully as you play so that the volume increases or decreases note by note right up to the final sound.

Accent Types

Accents can have different meanings and also different sound levels. Look for clues to an accent's meaning in the piece's title, tempo marking, the dynamics around the accent, and the phrase it occurs in.

An accent in a *piano* section should sound totally different from an accent in a *forte* section. An accent can be sudden and forceful, but it can also be expressive, more like the emphasis you hear when a violinist adds vibrato to a sound.

Vary the suddenness and loudness of your accent by altering the speed of your finger action and the amount of weight you use. The faster your finger strikes the key, the sharper the sound will be. And you can vary the effect of the accent or *sforzando* by using weight in different ways. Try each of the following movements on an accent and listen to the different results.

- Use only the weight of your finger (for a *piano* accent, for example).

- Snap your wrist.

- Thrust your arm forward from the elbow.

- Use the weight of your whole arm from the shoulder.

You can also emphasize a note by playing it slightly late. This is called an agogic accent.

Overview

When you are polishing or reviewing a piece, look beyond the small details and think about the piece as a whole. What does this music say to you, and how can you convey that meaning to others? Here are some questions to consider. Search your score to find the answers, and use them to deepen your performance.

- Where is the climax of the piece? How do you know that this is the most important moment? At what point should you start building up to it?

- How many measures or sections or pages of the piece are basically soft? What mood or moods should they convey?

- When you record yourself, can you hear the high points? Do your soft sounds contrast dramatically with surrounding loud sounds?

- What is the overall mood of the piece, or does it change moods? Can you hear that in your playing?

Tuck Under

When you strike a key on a piano, its hammer hits the strings and sets them vibrating. But as soon as the hammer bounces away, the string vibrations become smaller and smaller, causing the sound to fade away.

After playing a long note, listen carefully as its sound decreases. Blend the next note into this natural *diminuendo* by playing the second note softer than the first. Unless you tuck under in this way, your melody line will be bumpy.

Play figure 12.1 with every note *forte*. Play again, but this time tuck under the note that follows the dotted note. Notice how much smoother the melody sounds now.

Fig. 12.1. Tchaikovsky, Old French Song.

Tchaikovsky

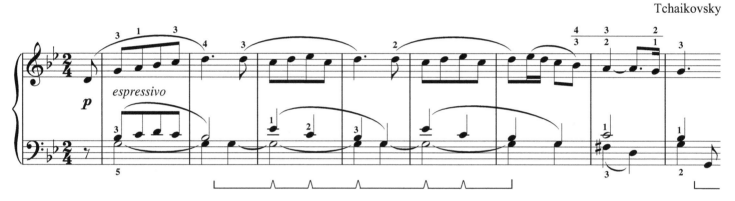
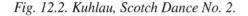

Follow this principle even during a *crescendo*. Figure 12.2, for example, shows a *crescendo* extending over four measures. Here the quarter note is the long note. Instead of making every single note louder than the previous note, tuck under after B♭ and again after B natural, then *crescendo* up to C. You will still have a *crescendo*, but the effect will be more musical than if you had played every single note louder than the last one.

Fig. 12.2. Kuhlau, Scotch Dance No. 2.

Kuhlau

72

Creative Repetition

Repeated notes can sound boring or bangy, or they can make a piece come alive. They might be dramatic or funny or suspenseful. They might move the music to a climax or taper it off delicately. They might be boisterous or graceful.

Play the excerpts in figures 12.3 through 12.6 to appreciate the variety of effects that repeated notes can provide. In the Beethoven Sonatina (fig. 12.3), the repeated notes move forward, so make a small *crescendo* over each bar line.

Fig. 12.3. Beethoven, Sonatina in G Major.

Beethoven

In Mozart's Minuet (fig. 12.4), however, the repeated notes should be graceful and softer than the downbeat to enhance the dance character, so make a small *diminuendo* each time.

Fig. 12.4. Mozart, Minuet in F.

Mozart

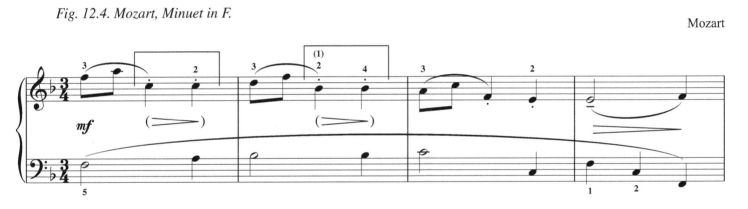

Composers also use repeated notes to create a mood. The crisp, soft chords in the introduction to Burgmüller's Etude (fig. 12.5) instantly establish the highly rhythmic and *scherzando* quality of the piece.

Fig. 12.5 Burgmüller, Etude, Op. 100, No. 2.

Burgmüller

In contrast, Beethoven's repeated notes in the middle section of *Für Elise* (fig. 12.6) have a mysterious, almost ominous quality that completely alters the mood of the piece.

Fig. 12.6. Beethoven, Für Elise.

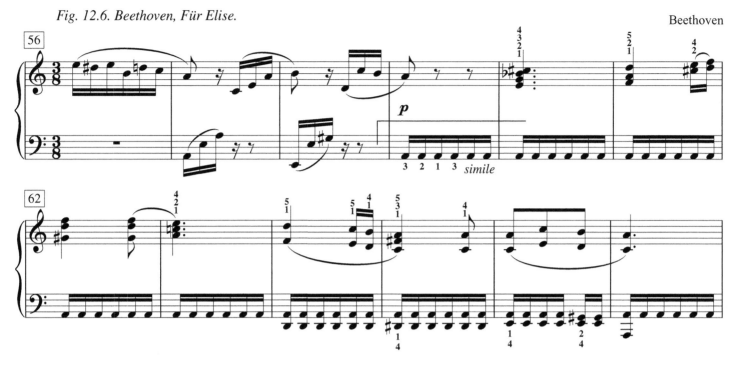

Play each set of repeated notes in your piece with an appropriate meaning. Use dynamics to give a sense of forward motion (*crescendo*) or relaxation (*diminuendo*).

Cello Lines

Most piano music has the melody in the right hand, so much of our attention naturally goes to making the right hand sing. But composers write beautiful melodies for the left hand, too, even though the main melody is elsewhere. Play the example below just as expressively as you would play a solo melody.

It probably didn't sound familiar, yet it belongs to one of the best known melodies in piano literature (fig. 12.7).

Fig. 12.7. J.S. Bach, Minuet in G Major.

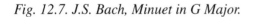

Look for melodies like this in your own piece. Pretend that you are playing the cello and that this is the only melody you get to play because the violin has the main melody. If you really were a cellist, you'd try to make your melody just as beautiful as, but softer than, the violin's.

Other times the left hand has a part that may not sound like a singing melody, but that steers the music by outlining harmonic changes (fig. 12.8). This kind of a bass line provides a solid foundation for the melody. It's just as important to music as a foundation is to a building. Even though we play the melody prominently, we still want it to have a strong foundation.

Fig. 12.8. Mozart, Minuet in F, K2.

Mozart

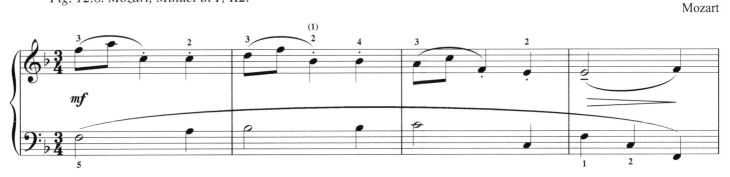

Three in a Row

Search through your piece for motifs or phrases that happen three times in a row. A motif might be as small as two or three notes. Or you might find a half measure, a measure, or a whole phrase that appears three times, either exactly the same (repetition) or almost the same (sequence, imitation).

Never play all three groups the same way. Make each group sound fresh by increasing the volume, diminishing it, making an echo, using the pedal, changing the articulation. If you listen to how the harmony affects the melody, you may get an idea of a good way to vary the sound.

BALANCE AND VOICING

One reason people enjoy playing the piano is that, unlike most other instruments, it can make many sounds at once. For these simultaneous sounds to make sense, however, the pianist has to layer them, making some sounds stand out more than others.

In everyday usage the word balance has to do with equality. In music, however, balance actually means unequal. Because pianists typically play at least two lines of music at a time, and often three or four, finding the proper balance (meaning, really, *im*balance) is critical. The main melody must stand out, secondary melodies must complement it, accompaniments must adorn, and bass lines must provide a foundation. And everything must be heard!

The minute a piece calls for playing two hands at once, the job of layering, or voicing, begins. First determine which is the main melody. Then the question is, how do I make that part stand out? And the answer is, dynamics: play the melody louder than marked while playing its accompaniment softer than marked.

We have an even bigger challenge when one hand must play two melodies simultaneously. While it is easier to play double melodies on a piano than on, say, a violin (and you can't do it at all on most instruments), the challenge is to play multiple voices in such a way that each one makes sense. Especially when two voices are close to each other, it's hard to hear them as two independent melodies. When played at the same dynamic level, two lines are difficult to hear. They may even cancel each other out.

So a pianist must learn to layer sounds. The following tips will help you achieve good musical balance.

Good Balance Formula

Composers usually put a single dynamic mark in the space between treble and bass clef. That does not mean, however, that every note within a section marked *forte* should be loud. Figure 12.9 shows a melody in the left hand accompanied by right-hand chords. The dynamic marking is *piano*. To achieve an overall *piano* sound, play the melody one dynamic level louder (*mezzo piano*) and the accompaniment one level softer (*pianissimo*). Together these sounds will produce a general effect of *piano* ($p = mp + pp$).

Fig. 12.9. Burgmüller, Etude, Op. 100, No. 15.

Burgmüller

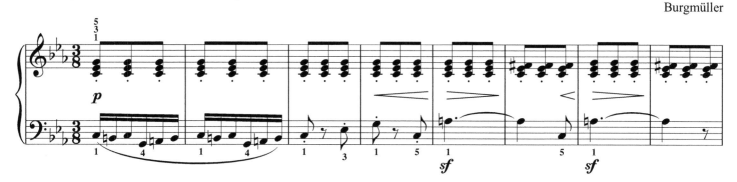

Use the same formula for good balance at any other dynamic level.

General effect of mp = mf (melody) + p (accompaniment)

General effect of mf = f (melody) + mp (accompaniment)

General effect of f = ff (melody) + mf (accompaniment)

Change the formula if you like to make your layering more dramatic, but keep the principle intact.

Balancing Act

1. Pick one phrase of the piece and play the main melody alone, *forte*.

2. Play the accompaniment alone, *pianissimo*.

3. Put the two parts together, listening for the same big difference in sound levels.

4. Play with your hands two or three octaves apart, balanced in the same way.

5. Play cross-handed, balanced in the same way.

Ghosts

Play the melody with a big, singing tone at the same time that you play the accompaniment like a ghost—fingers moving, but completely silent. When you can do this easily, add a tiny bit of sound (*pianissimo*) to the accompaniment and play that along with the melody. Listen carefully: the melody should still have a big, singing sound, and the accompaniment should still be no more than a ghostly whisper.

Hidden Melodies

Great composers write interesting, even beautiful, accompaniment figures. Figure 12.10 shows a typical example. The hidden melody in the left hand accompaniment moves parallel to the main melody in the right hand. There is a repeated G inserted between each hidden melody tone in the left hand.

Fig. 12.10. Schumann, Melody, Op. 68, No. 1.

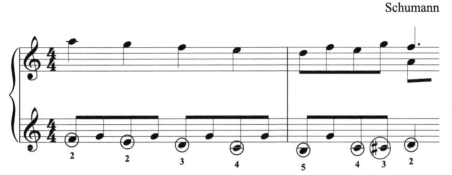

As simple as these measures look, they require thoughtful practice to play well. Try the following steps on figure 12.10, and then apply them to similar passages in your piece.

1. Play the main melody alone. Decide how you want to shape it, and play it that way.

2. Find the hidden melody in the accompaniment and play it, leaving out the repeating notes. Shape it just like the main melody, but softer.

3. Combine the main melody and the hidden melody (still without the repeating notes), and play them together, with the main melody one level louder than the secondary melody.

4. Work on the accompaniment alone. Play all notes, but make the hidden melody notes one level louder than the repeating notes. (Drop some weight into the melody notes and keep your fingers very light on the repeating notes.)

5. Put everything together. Play the main melody *mezzo forte*, the hidden melody *mezzo piano*, and the repeating notes *pianissimo*.

Double Duty

Sometimes one hand is given several things to do at once. This could happen horizontally (fig. 12.11) or vertically (fig. 12.12).

Fig. 12.11. Burgmüller, Etude, Op. 100, No. 7.

Fig. 12.12. Tchaikovsky, The Doll's Funeral.

Tchaikovsky

In figure 12.11 the right hand plays both a melody (shown by the quarter note down stems) and an accompaniment (triplet eighth notes). In figure 12.12 the right hand plays two melodies simultaneously.

Separate the voices to discover how each one sounds by itself.

1. Play each voice with one hand. Use any fingering as long as it allows you to play legato. (Check the direction of each note stem. The notes with up stems belong to one voice, and the notes with down stems belong to another.)

2. Decide which melody is more important.

3. Play the two voices with two hands. Make the main melody *forte* and the secondary melody (or accompaniment) *pianissimo*. Repeat several times to get the sound in your ear.

4. Now play the two voices with one hand, as written in the music. This should sound just as it did when you used two hands. Repeat five times.

Chord Voicing

Pianists must learn to "voice" chords. Whenever one hand plays two or more notes at once—double notes or chords—a choice has to be made. Which of the notes should sound louder than the others? With chords in the right hand, it is usually the top note. Sometimes a composer even shows us, by using special stems, which notes to bring out. Think of the top line, or up stems, as a melody and the other notes of the chord as accompaniment.

1. Play the top line *forte* with your right hand while playing the other chord tones *pianissimo* with your left hand. Repeat five or six times. You should be able to hear the melody singing out above the accompaniment.

2. Next play all the notes with your right hand. Imagine that you are carrying a weight, like a bean bag, on the outer part of your right hand and that this weight flows through your fingers into the piano keys. Imagine that the thumb side of your right hand is floating on the keys.

3. Now you have the sound in your ear and the physical sensation in your hand. Try playing the whole chord sequence. Does the melody still ring out? Keep trying until it does. It's fine to go back to two hands every once in a while, just to remind yourself how you want it to sound.

MUSICAL PHRASING

Remember that the way you shape a phrase tells the listener what the music means. It is important, therefore, to review where each phrase begins and ends, to decide on a dynamic shape for it, and to think about how each phrase fits into the musical whole.

Phrase Meaning

Look at a section of your piece. How many phrases does it contain? Play each phrase by itself and then answer these questions:

- Are there two identical, or almost identical, phrases?

- Which phrase sounds most dramatic?

- Is there a phrase that contains a surprise?

- Is one phrase totally different from the others?

- Which phrase is your favorite?

You can highlight special qualities of a phrase by changing dynamics, by taking a little extra time, or by using more or less pedal or a different type of articulation.

Sound Stretches

Although an octave leap takes considerable energy for a flutist or for a singer, all a pianist has to do is press down two keys. Large intervals are so easily played on the piano that we sometimes forget how much they mean in a musical phrase.

If your melody contains a skip larger than a fifth, sing the interval a few times. Feel your vocal chords stretching for the higher pitch. Notice the effort it takes to move your voice from one note to the other. When you play this melody on the piano, try to get the same effect, as though you were reaching for the second sound.

Quicksand

It can be difficult to maintain a slow tempo. Use your imagination to help sustain a *largo* or *adagio* tempo. Imagine, for example, that each key you play is like quicksand: it holds your finger and tries to keep it from moving on to the next key.

Mood Music

Change the mood of your piece or a section of your piece. Make it sound:

happy, then sad
silly, then serious
wild, then careful
funny, then solemn
brave, then scared
mysterious, then certain
angry, then kind
worried, then calm
tragic, then ridiculous

What did you actually do to create these different moods? You may have changed

the speed,
the dynamics,
the timing,
the articulation,
the pedal, or just
the way you felt inside.

Between the Notes

This tip is especially good for slow pieces. Play one phrase at a time, melody alone. Start by listening to the sound (or the silence) between the notes. Ask yourself:

1. What happens in the space between two notes? Does one note grow into the next or relax into it? Should the second note be a surprise or more of the same? Show that in your playing.

2. Imagine—silently sing—a melody as you play it on the piano. From one note to the next, can you feel the change inside of you—an opening up, for example, or a calming down, or a surprise?

Tick Tock

When you play with the metronome, make sure that your melody is smooth, whether you play on the ticks or in between them. Follow the metronome's pulse, but keep the melodic line independent. Listen for long phrases, and don't allow accents on the metronome ticks.

Phrase Counts

Once you have reached the desired tempo of a fast piece, you probably are not counting beats any more. Try counting phrases instead, as in figure 12.13.

If you have written the counts into each measure, erase those numbers and replace them with one number per measure. Use one count for each measure, and start the count over when a new phrase begins. As you play, ask yourself if each phrase is shaped the way you want it.

Fig. 12.13. Burgmüller, Etude, Op. 100, No. 2.

Burgmüller

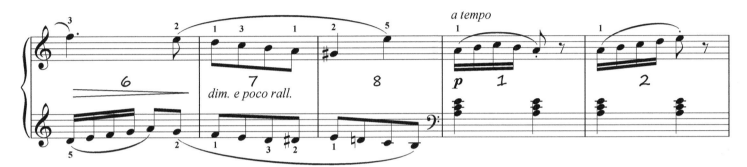

EFFECTIVE PEDALING

Devote some time to pedaling in every practice session, either by simply listening carefully to the pedal effect as you play or by using some of the following practice tips.

Pedal Connection

Play through your piece and focus your attention on the pedaling. Listen carefully each time you change the pedal. What do you hear? A space? Two sounds blurred together? Or smoothly connected sounds?

If you hear a space, it means you are lifting the pedal too soon. If you hear two sounds blurred together, it means you are lifting the pedal too soon and probably putting it down again too soon as well. To deal with either of these problems, see **Pedal Counts** (Chapter 8). If you hear one sound blending cleanly into another, you know your pedaling is perfect.

Pedal Depth

The damper pedal can make music sound watery. How watery, though, is up to you. Play figure 12.14. Every time you pedal, press the damper pedal to the floor.

Fig. 12.14. Chopin, Waltz, Op. 64, No.1.

Chopin

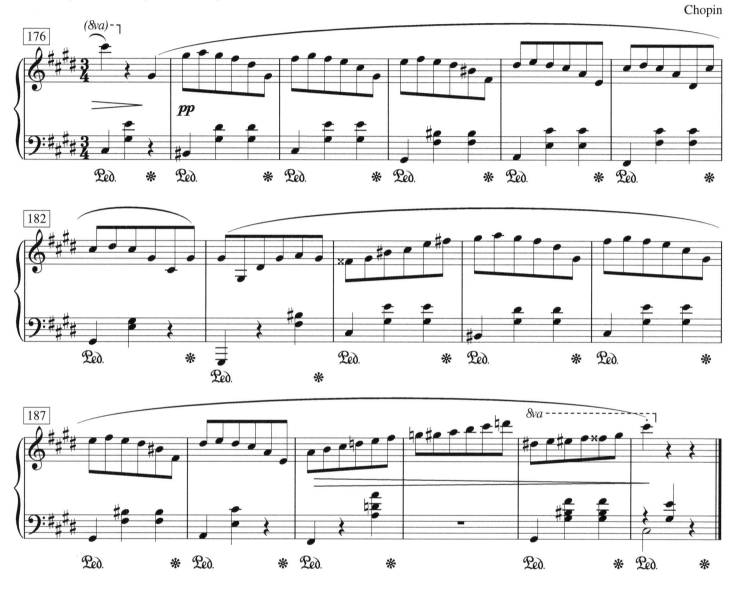

Repeat, but this time put the pedal only halfway down. Repeat again, this time pressing the pedal down only an inch. Decide which way the music sounds best. The next time you use the pedal, remember the different sounds you can get by pressing it down all the way, halfway, or only a tiny amount.

If you have ever driven a car, you could think of the pedal the way you think of a car's accelerator. Barely pressing the pedal would be like going 5 miles per hour, pressing it down halfway like going 30 miles per hour, and pressing it to the floor like going 60 miles per hour.

Pedal Effect

Don't let your foot movements affect your musical line. Sometimes, without realizing it, pianists make an accent every time they change the pedal. Listen carefully to be sure that your melodic line is smooth no matter how many pedal changes you make.

Hidden Pedal

Pedaling should not show. Except when you play a mood piece using long pedals for special effects, no one should realize that you are pedaling. There are two kinds of sound to hide when you pedal: blurred harmonies and mechanical thumps.

1. Put your hands in your lap. Play the pedal all by itself, following the marks in your piece and in the normal tempo of the piece. (You may want to use the metronome to keep you on track.)

2. What do you hear from under the piano? Do you hear your shoe slapping the pedal? Does the pedal thump when you release it? Both of these noises will disappear if you keep your foot touching the pedal. Imagine that your shoe is glued to the pedal, especially when you have to change the pedal quickly.

3. Once you are sure there is no mechanical noise, add the notes, one hand at a time. Listen for clarity and whatever effect you desire—to connect, to enhance the sound, to increase the volume.

4. After you've practiced the piece with pedal long enough to be comfortable with it, record yourself and listen to the recording to be sure your pedaling is clean.

Backpedal

After you feel comfortable pedaling a piece or a section of a piece, play it entirely without pedal every few days to make sure you are still playing legato.

Nonpedal

Some people have a hard time *not* pedaling, even when they know they shouldn't pedal, or when their teacher has advised them not to. If inadvertent pedaling happens to you, slide your right foot *under* the pedal while you practice, so that it won't press the pedal down without receiving intentional commands from you.

End Pedal

If you use pedal at the end of your piece, be sure to do so in a way that will enhance the mood. Figures 12.15 and 12.16 show the ending of two Burgmüller etudes. You can make the first ending more exciting by lifting the pedal suddenly. The second one, however, calls for the pedal to be released a bit at a time so that the dreamy mood is not broken abruptly.

Fig. 12.15. Burgmüller, Etude, Op. 100, No. 2.

Fig. 12.16. Burgmüller, Etude, Op. 100, No. 21.

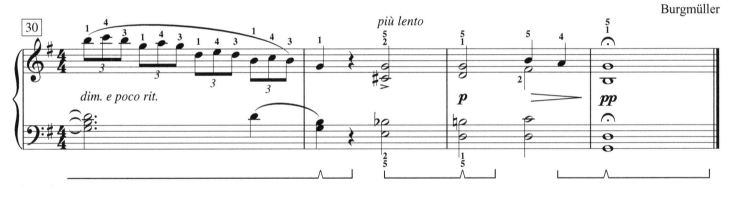

Once a piece is polished the question arises, "What next?" You may wish to memorize it, or to perform it for friends or a broader public, or to maintain it in your repertoire as you turn to your next project.

Chapter 13 gives general advice on memorization plus specific strategies for memorizing a piece thoroughly and efficiently. Chapter 14 suggests how to prepare for a successful performance by channeling the natural excitement that comes with playing before an audience. Chapter 15 offers ideas on how to keep a piece that has been learned, polished, and loved in your repertoire and in your fingers when it's time to move on to new pieces.

CHAPTER 13
MEMORIZING MUSIC

I have heard master teachers say that if you practice correctly, your piece will be memorized. They mean that if you understand a piece of music thoroughly (Start Smart, Chapter 1) and if you practice challenging portions diligently (e.g., practice tips), you will automatically commit the piece to memory.

I think this is 100 percent true for some people, but less so for others. Certainly if you have practiced effectively you can play parts of your piece without the music. To memorize the entire piece, though, most students of the piano need specific strategies.

There are many ways of remembering music—how it feels, how it sounds, how it looks, what you know about it. When a piece is four or eight measures long, it can be memorized almost immediately. Young beginners typically remember and perform their short pieces with ease. But when pieces get longer and more complicated and when children grow older and become more self-conscious, it takes more time and effort to memorize music. Many adults say that facility in memorizing decreases with age.

Even when memorization is done with care, it doesn't work perfectly all the time. You may memorize something one day but forget it the next. Small or large memory slips can occur in performance. These slips happen to everyone, even the greatest performing artists. But because experienced musicians know how to cover up a slip, their audiences usually remain unaware of the problem.

Some people never have trouble remembering their pieces in performance, other people do. Some people go for years without memory problems, and suddenly one day they have a memory lapse in a performance.

There is no cure for memory slips, but everyone can become better at covering up memory slips through frequent practice performances and learning to keep going no matter what happens. Whether memorizing is hard or easy for you, don't take it for granted. The following practice tips help make memory more secure. Do one or two a day, and mix them up to keep it interesting.

MEMORIZATION STRATEGIES

When you start memorizing a piece, especially a long piece, it's important to organize your practicing. This may keep you from feeling overwhelmed.

Review what you learned from mapping the piece when you began to study it. If the form of the piece is *ABA* with a slight change in the second *A* section, for example, find the circle you made around that change. Since all the *A* material before that circle is the same as the first *A* section, all you need to memorize is the circled spot and whatever comes right before and after it.

In other words, before you start memorizing a piece, make sure you know which phrases or sections are exact repeats of prior material and therefore do not need your attention. You might even cross out those parts very lightly in pencil, or you could flag them with removable color tape. It's always nice to see how much work you *don't* have to do.

Pianists often memorize both hands at once, especially when they've been playing a piece long enough to be familiar with it. This approach seems natural, but it has an important drawback. Hands-together memorizing tends to result in good right-hand memory (supported by the ear, which remembers the melody) and weak left-hand memory. The left hand simply follows the right hand, like a puppy on a leash. The left hand probably cannot play by itself.

This is dangerous, because nearly all memory slips in performance are failures of the left hand. You can reduce memory slips by memorizing music hands separately: your memory will be much more dependable.

Memory Calendar

1. Count the measures (in a short piece) or the phrases (in a long piece).

2. Divide the number of measures or phrases by the number of practice days until your next lesson to see how much you need to memorize each day.

3. Write the due dates in your music. It's best to start at the end of the piece, not the beginning (see **Back Up** in Chapter 4—the same reasoning holds here). Allow yourself more time for sections you think will be hard to memorize. Some phrases may already be in your memory: let your calendar goals reflect this too.

4. Don't expect to remember something after "memorizing" it once. Repeat each newly memorized section five or ten times before going on.

5. Save the last day of your practice week for review—no new material that day.

Memory Steps

Choose one phrase to memorize. Look at the music and play the phrase four times, hands separately. Do the left hand first, then the right hand. Each time you play, do something different:

1. Sing the count.

2. Sing the finger numbers.

3. Sing the note names.

4. Listen to the dynamics.

Repeat each task without the music. When you feel ready, put hands together and do steps 1 and 4. If you stumble, do these two steps with the music, and then try again without the music.

Finger Memory

Finger slips cause memory slips. One day you might be happily playing along from memory and suddenly finger 3 plays a note that is usually played by finger 2. Now the fingering pattern has been disturbed, and a memory lapse may follow. If your fingers get lost, so do you.

So when you are memorizing a piece, don't look only at the notes and the rhythm—memorize the fingering as well. Say the finger numbers aloud as you play, first with the music—just as you did when you first learned the piece—and then without the music.

Words to Remember

Make up words to your music—words that fit the music and help you remember it. For example, here are some words for Turk's March in G Major (fig. 13.1):

> *Hop, hop, hop to the A below,*
>
> *Then go walking up to Dee-ee.*
>
> *Hop again to the A below,*
>
> *Slide to B, then to A, then to Gee-ee.*

Fig. 13.1. Turk, March in G Major.

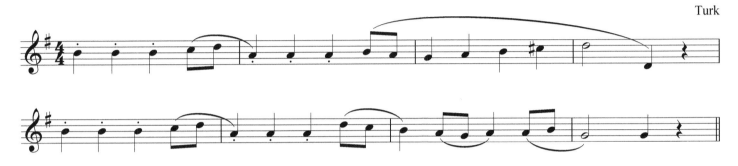

Notice that these words not only mention specific notes in the music; they also suggest articulation ("hop" for staccato, "walk" and "slide" for legato). And the word "again" highlights the music's repetition.

Sing-Along

Play the accompaniment while singing the melody, first with the music and then without.

Memory Markers

Once you believe your piece is memorized, label each section with a number. Play from any one of these markers to the end of the piece, first with the music and then without the music.

For an extra challenge, play from the beginning up to a certain number, skip forward to another number and continue to play from there to the end. For example, if you numbered the sections, play up to number 3 and then skip to number 5 and finish the piece.

Baroque Memory

When memorizing a contrapuntal piece such as a Bach invention or fugue (also some preludes and dance movements), memorize one voice at a time, not one hand at a time (because one voice may move from one hand to the other).

TESTING MEMORY

Nonmusicians are often amazed to hear a pianist play from memory. ("How can you possibly remember all those notes?") They are right, playing from memory requires long and careful preparation followed by immense concentration during the actual performance. You have done the preparation; now use the following tips to test and improve your concentration. Try a variety of strategies, because each one will stretch a different part of your brain.

One-Handed Memory

Test your single-handed memory:

- Play through your whole piece without the music, one hand at a time. You can work up to this by doing it one phrase at a time.

- At your lesson, play one hand from memory while your teacher plays the other.

Where Am I?

Ask someone to stop you at various points as you play your piece from memory. When you are stopped, name the key you are in and the section of the piece (*A*, *B*, first theme, etc.).

Paper Memory

Write out your piece, or a part of it, on manuscript paper without looking at the original or playing it. Listen to the music in your imagination, and then write it down. Play it to see if you remembered everything.

Mixed Media Memory

Try the following on one or two phrases or even the whole piece.

Play both hands, but with only one hand on the keys. "Play" the other hand on the ledge above the keyboard, on your lap, on your knee, on your piano bench. Reverse the hands. Finally, play both hands on the keyboard. It should seem easier than before.

If you can do this without the music, your memory is very secure.

Dynamic Memory

You may have memorized the notes and rhythms, but do you know your dynamics? Find out by writing out the dynamic map of your piece. Figure 13.2 is a dynamic map of an excerpt from Duncombe's Fanfare in C Major (see fig. 1.1).

Fig. 13.2. Dynamic map of the Duncombe Fanfare.

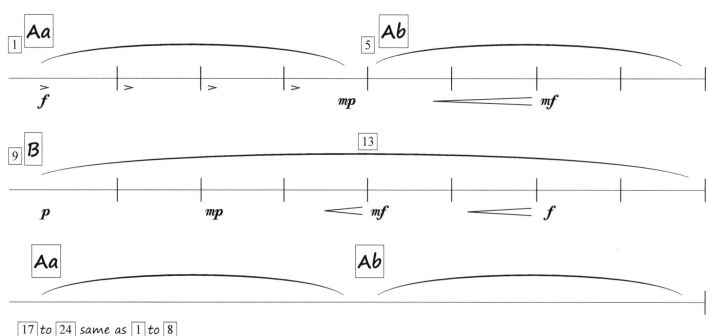

Blindfold

Play from memory with your eyes closed. It's okay to peek in spots where your hands have to make a major position change; then close your eyes again.

Ottline Memory

Do the following on one phrase at a time and then see if you can extend it to two phrases, a whole section, or even the entire piece.

First with the music and then without it, play only the notes that fall on the main beats of each measure. Or play all notes of the melody part but only the main beats of the accompaniment.

Doing this successfully suggests that your memory is solid. Even if you do have a problem in performance, though, you will recover quickly because you will remember what that next Ottline is.

Spot Check

Close your eyes and drop your finger on a spot in the music. Open your eyes and look where your finger landed. Close the book and play from that spot to the end with notes, rhythm, and dynamics in place.

Half-Time Memory

Play your piece from memory at half speed.

Dropouts

While playing through part of your piece from memory, drop out the right hand, but continue to play with left hand. Repeat, but this time drop out the left hand and continue to play with the right hand.

CHAPTER 14
PREPARING TO PERFORM

The best way to go into a performance with confidence is to prepare for it with effective, thoughtful, thorough practicing. In fact, for well-prepared performers, having an audience can actually cause the performance to be better than it ever was in the practice room. Nevertheless, performing is totally different from practicing, so it calls for special preparation.

Playing for an audience, or even the thought of a coming performance, normally causes a release of adrenaline into the blood system. Adrenaline is a hormone and neurotransmitter produced by the body when the central nervous system experiences excitement, fear, anxiety, or exhilaration. Adrenaline causes the body to feel different. Some people get cold hands, others get sweaty palms. The heart rate increases, which causes performers to be highly alert, even jumpy.

That jumpy condition is often called "butterflies." It feels as if butterflies are flitting around in your stomach and chest. Butterflies may start days before a performance and can put into motion a destructive spiral of anxiety. Banish the butterflies by taking long, deep breaths and shifting your thoughts to something other than the upcoming performance.

Keep your life, and your mind, orderly in the time leading up to a performance:

- If you are playing several pieces in a performance, plan the order in advance. Start, or end, with the one that you like the best or play the best.

- Select comfortable clothes for the performance, and practice in them before the performance. Pay special attention to shoes. You may be planning to perform in new shoes or shoes that you haven't worn much. Practice pedaling in them the week before the performance, so that there won't be any surprises. Even better, wear those shoes to practice on the performance piano.

- On the day of the performance, do everything slowly. Move slowly, talk slowly, breathe slowly, eat slowly. And above all, practice slowly.

- Never test your memory or your technique on performance day. Keep the music in front of you at the piano and play so slowly that you cannot possibly make a mistake.

- Allow extra time to get to the performance—running late causes anxiety.

- Remember that performing is giving great music to other people, usually to people who do not play themselves. Focus on one person in the audience—a parent, a friend, even a stranger—and imagine that person loving the music you play and leaving the room happier because of your gift.

Here are some practice tips that are especially useful in the final weeks before a performance.

Imagination Station
Everyone gets nervous when performing, whether it's playing the piano, giving a presentation in school or at work or taking an exam. Use your powers of imagination to reduce performance anxiety.

- When you are practicing at home for a performance, imagine yourself in the performance space. Paint the picture in detail: the stage, the lighting, and the color of the walls; the kind of bench you'll sit on; the size, color, brand, and position of the piano; the friends, adjudicators, family, or strangers who might be in the audience—whatever thing or person you expect to be there.

- When you are actually in the performance space, turn the whole process around. Picture yourself at home practicing. Again, "see" everything in the room, "hear" the sounds of home, feel the comfort of a safe place.

Piano Hopping
There are many advantages in choosing the piano as your instrument, but one distinct disadvantage is that you can't carry it with you.

Every piano feels and sounds different, so when you are preparing for a performance, get ready by playing your piece on as many different pianos as you can find. Go to a piano store's showroom, for example, or your neighbor's house. If your teacher has two pianos, take your lesson on the piano that you don't normally use. And, of course, if possible arrange to practice at least once on the piano you'll use in performance.

Three S's
Play slow, soft, and short (not staccato, just gently detached). This is a good way to lower anxiety when practicing a difficult passage or on the day of a performance. Your playing should sound and feel calm.

Check Your Pulse
With a partner following along in the score, play through your piece or any section of your piece from memory, counting silently as you play. Ask your partner to stop you seven or eight times. Each time you are stopped, tell your partner which count of the measure you are on. (Don't do this on your performance day, though.)

Setting the Pace

Once you know how fast or slow you want your piece to be, practice setting the tempo. Take 30 seconds before beginning the piece to imagine the first few phrases. As you do this, keep a strong pulse alive inside you. If it's a piece that you have trouble keeping steady or a piece that you don't feel totally comfortable with yet, think about the hardest phrase of the piece. What speed is comfortable for you there? Use this beat as your beginning pulse.

The metronome can be helpful in calming you down in the days leading up to a performance. Simply set it at the desired speed and play through the piece with the metronome as your partner. If possible, use only one tick per measure, which will allow you to play more freely between downbeats.

Ten, Nine, Eight...

Before you begin to play a piece in performance or in a practice performance, follow these steps to make yourself comfortable, to clear your mind, and to set your concentration:

1. Sit down. If necessary, adjust the bench height and distance from the piano.

2. Check the distance to the pedal. Your heel needs to rest on the floor when your foot is on the pedal.

3. Put your hands in your lap and count backwards slowly from ten to one. It has to be backwards, not forwards. (As my teacher Margaret Ott explained it, "backwards counting gets rid of the noise in your brain.")

4. Hear the first few phrases of your piece in your imagination.

5. Play.

CHAPTER 15
OLD REPERTOIRE

If you have a piece that's been learned and polished and you still love it but you have new pieces to practice, you can either put it away for awhile or you can keep it on the back burner.

If you plan to perform this piece again in the future, it's a very good idea to let it rest for some weeks or months. When you pick it up again, you may be amazed how easily it comes back to you. In fact, don't be surprised if you play it better the second time around. The mind has a wonderful way of continuing to work on projects that we think we've put to bed.

Here are three practice tips on returning to an old piece and one (***Rep Box***) on how to keep old pieces in your fingers.

Opposites Attract 2
So that you can hear and feel the music in a new way, do the following variation of ***Opposites Attract*** (Chapter 7). If the passage is

- legato, play it staccato and vice versa

- mostly *broken chords*, play them *blocked*, and vice versa

- *forte*, play it *piano*, and vice versa

- *fast*, play it *slow*, and vice versa

- supposed to *crescendo*, make a *diminuendo*, and vice versa.

Speed Trials
Using the metronome as a guide, play your piece, or a section of it, at three different speeds—regular speed, five notches slower, and half speed.

Separation
Take a piece or a section of a piece that you can play well hands together and practice it hands separate again. If the piece calls for pedal, play once without pedal and once with pedal.

Rep Box

- Decide which pieces you want to preserve.

- Write the name of each piece and its composer and any other relevant information (date of completion or performance, etc.) on a 3 x 5 index card.

- Put the cards into an index card box and keep this box on or near your piano.

- Every day, pick one card and play through that piece. A good way to do this is to pick the front card. After you've played the piece you file that card in the back. The next day you pick the front card again and so on.

Throughout the years of a child's music study, most communication will be two-way—between teacher and parent, or parent and child, or teacher and child. Each person has a role to play, and the roles should complement one another. This section offers some advice to parents and to teachers, ending with some observations on the practice triangle: how teacher, student, and parent can interact to enhance the practice experience.

CHAPTER 16
PARENTS' ROLE IN PRACTICING

When parents start a child in music, they usually have more in mind than entertainment. They are not thinking in terms of a year or two of amusement at the piano. Rather, they imagine their child growing into an adult who can sit down at the piano any time, anywhere, and play for pleasure. This chapter offers ideas for parents on all the aspects of early lessons—the instrument, the teacher, the lesson, and practicing.

THE INSTRUMENT

Before lessons begin no one knows whether a child's interest in music will become an enjoyable pastime, blossom into a lifelong passion, or fizzle out in six months. This uncertainty leads many parents to limit their horizons to the least expensive instrument and the nearest teacher, choices that may lay the foundation for failure.

Students should begin piano lessons on an acoustic piano, not an electronic piano. In the first year of lessons, teachers work on what is called "building the hand," which means developing a strong "roof," or top of the hand and a strong first joint of each finger. These qualities make finger independence possible, and finger independence is the basis of facility on the piano.

The process of building strength into the hand requires resistance from an instrument's keys—the finger and the key are opposing forces. Because the keys of electronic instruments are easier to depress than the keys of an acoustic piano, an electronic instrument requires less strength and digital facility than an acoustic piano. For that reason, practicing on an electronic instrument doesn't build a strong hand structure, and most children who start out practicing this way start at a disadvantage. Later, if they switch to an acoustic piano, there will be readjustment and rebuilding that may prove tedious, which is not a quality that anyone wants in piano lessons.

Invest as much as you can afford in a piano so that you will have an instrument that sounds good and stays in tune. You will have to pay for quality, but fortunately pianos have excellent resale value. Most grand pianos are superior to most upright pianos, but there are exceptions.

There are a number of excellent books on purchasing new and used pianos to inform your choice. If you are not in a hurry and have the ability to pay full price up front, consider buying a used piano. You can often get a great value this way. Just be sure to bring in a registered piano technician to give you an expert assessment of any piano you think you might buy.

THE TEACHER

Look for high quality in selecting a teacher for your beginner. Get the best you can afford—and if you can't afford the best, seek scholarship assistance. The first year of lessons may be the most important year of all. Your child is excited and ready for a new adventure. A great teacher at this point can set the stage for a lifetime of musical endeavor; an inadequate teacher can put out the flame.

Your child deserves to start piano with an experienced, knowledgeable, respected, personable teacher. So don't limit yourself to the closest teacher or the one with the lowest rates. Ask your friends, read local teachers' web sites and attend teachers' student piano recitals. Keep in mind that not all excellent teachers are good with beginners. If the best teacher in town has no students your child's age, that might not be the best choice for you.

If there are several likely choices in your area, set up an interview with each one of them (expect to pay a fee for this). The interview is a three-way interaction. The teacher will work with your child to get an impression of personality, musical aptitude, and general readiness. Each teacher will handle this in a different way, and your child will probably react accordingly, which should give you a good idea of where the best fit lies. You may ask the teacher questions about methods or philosophy of teaching. The teacher will likely have questions for you as well. Throughout the process, all three of you are forming an impression of how well you might work together over the long-term. This is important: good chemistry counts.

If the cost of the teacher you want is beyond your means, schedule an interview anyway and inquire about financial aid. Experienced teachers appreciate parents who have a serious commitment to music study, and they are often willing to make financial sacrifices for children from this kind of family.

Look for a teacher who requires summer lessons—maybe not every week, but at least five or six times while school is out. Children who spend the whole summer without lessons (and practicing) lose a lot. It will take them several months in the fall to recover the knowledge that has slipped away. Then, too, summer is a more relaxed time, with more available hours in the day, so it only makes sense to use that period for musical growth.

It's also worthwhile making an effort to attend prospective teachers' piano recitals. Teachers usually welcome guests at their studio recitals (although you should inquire first just to be sure). When you go, notice whether or not there are students of your child's age, how well prepared the children are overall, and how they interact with each other and the teacher. Does the teacher create an atmosphere that would suit your child? Do you like the music you hear? What seems to be the spirit of the group of parents and children as a whole?

Choosing the best teacher does not mean that you, or the teacher, picture your child playing in Carnegie Hall. It simply means that you are committed enough to invest significant time, money, and emotional support over a period of years so that at the conclusion of lessons your child will be equipped to continue playing on her own (and if she turns out to be exceptional, maybe Carnegie Hall is in the cards after all).

THE LESSON

Lesson Length and Frequency

How much time will be devoted to each lesson, and how much time will be set aside for daily practicing? Biographies of legendary pianists often reveal a childhood teacher or sometimes a parent who made music with them every day of the week. If only each of us lived next door to a brilliant, loving musician, someone with the time and desire to sit with our children every day, to monitor their progress carefully, and to fill their lives with music—and if only we could afford it.

Instead, we drive our children to lessons—and not just piano lessons—struggling to fit them into tight schedules of our own and the teacher's. No one would dream of scheduling lessons every day. So we settle for lessons every week.

Children typically start piano with great excitement. They are like empty glasses waiting to be filled. Every lesson is an adventure, packed with new sounds and ideas. They love the attention from the new adult in their lives.

Make sure, however, that beginning lessons are not too short. Thirty-minute lessons would be fine if they happened every other day or even twice a week, but once-a-week lessons should be longer. There must be time for the teacher to listen to all the accomplishments of the week, to address any problems, and to present new material—not just new pieces but whole new concepts that require time to explain and demonstrate. This array of activities will require at least 45 minutes and more likely an hour.

Can a six- or seven-year-old handle this? Absolutely. But again, it is the teacher's creativity, experience, and personal skills that will make it work, so finding the right person is crucial.

Lessons with Parents

Generally, for the first several years of lessons, I ask parents to sit in on lessons and to supervise practice sessions. To facilitate this collaboration, we use several tools—a recording of the lesson, an assignment sheet, a practice guide,[2] and a practice schedule.

It's particularly important to me to have a parent observe lessons in the first year. I want parents to see what we do physically and understand why we do it, because those first 20 lessons or so set the stage for all future development. A watchful parent in the lesson is my best hope of having a child follow through correctly in daily practice.

The parent of one of my students expressed this concept perfectly: "I hear, see, and understand the teacher's instruction, so I can help my son in his daily practice."

Young students like having a parent in the lesson. I think it makes them feel important and I know they feel supported. One nine-year-old told me, "It's comforting to know my mom is there. Sometimes she asks questions so when we get home she can explain things to me if I forget or didn't completely understand."

Somewhere along the line, often when students reach middle school age, parents usually attend fewer lessons. Exactly when this happens varies according to the maturity of the child and the parent/child relationship. Sometimes even a child as young as nine or ten may start to function poorly in the parent's presence. In such a case I experiment with parentless lessons, an arrangement that may become permanent. But that's the exception rather than the rule.

By the time students are in high school I tell any parents who are still sitting in on lessons that, although they are welcome to attend an occasional lesson, they should no longer plan to be present regularly. By this time I expect students to be working more or less independently at home. I also believe that being alone with me in the lesson allows the student a kind of freedom that is crucial to his or her musical development.

Lessons without Parents

Some teachers prefer not to have parents attend lessons. In this case, the teacher may make sound or video recordings of the lessons or relevant portions of the lessons. This way parents will still have a clear understanding of the lesson and of what should follow in that week's practice sessions.

Parents tell me that recording a lesson is enormously helpful, whether they attend the lesson or not:

> "The recording gives us complete and accurate information from the lesson. I refer to it so that I can remind my son what to work on. I also show him how he can listen to some parts on his own. Once when he forgot to record I noticed that his practicing was much less efficient. So I make sure every lesson is recorded."

Another parent said,

> "I record the lesson with a video camera. I watch it one complete time before his first practice after the lesson. We watch together the parts that I think he forgot, especially when he needs to see how the teacher did something. We also watch it to resolve disagreements about instructions."

---

[2] Nancy O'Neill Breth, *The Parent's Guide to Effective Practicing* and *The Piano Student's Guide to Effective Practicing*, Hal Leonard Corporation.

Promoting Good Practice Habits

Managing a Child's Practicing

Establishing and maintaining the habit of daily practicing requires thought and careful planning. After all, we are asking children to be their own teachers for the six days between lessons. This is a level of independent study that no one else will require of them until they reach college. Is a young child capable of this kind of concentration, endurance, and patience? Yes, but it's tricky.

On one hand we have the power of a child's fascination with music and the piano, plus the child's desire to please both teacher and parents. On the other hand we have the introduction of a daily "homework" assignment that may require much more of the child than any school subject.

If a child is not ready for this amount of daily concentration, but shows interest in music, consider putting off private lessons and starting instead with a general music class where a child can build a strong foundation in essential musical principles while having fun with other children and having no "homework" obligation.

If you do opt for private lessons, set aside plenty of time each day for practicing. Even young beginners can practice 30 or 40 minutes a day or more if they have enough interesting tasks to complete. This may seem like a long time, but no one loves learning more than a young child—think of the endless repetitive actions of babies and toddlers as they learn to walk and talk. Learning piano is certainly no less interesting. And a skilled teacher knows how to challenge, but not overload, each student and how to select materials that will keep a child intrigued and always wanting more.

The importance of devoting more than a few minutes a day to piano practice cannot be overemphasized. Playing an instrument is different from listening to music. It requires the development of physical skills—just like learning a sport or ballet—and it takes daily training or workouts, or as we call it, practicing.

The most important goal in the early months of lessons is to set into motion a cycle of success. In this cycle the inspiration of the lesson leads to experimentation and learning in daily practicing, which leads to accomplishment, which leads to pleasure and pride, which leads into the next lesson.

There is a point early on in this process, usually sometime in the first year, when a student realizes not only that he is learning a lot, but that his level of accomplishment is directly related to how much and how well he practices. This student has entered the cycle of success.

If little or no time is devoted to the experimentation and learning phase, though, there won't be enough accomplishment to produce the satisfaction that makes practicing seem worthwhile. This is the moment when children become bored or frustrated and start to think of quitting. They may lose interest entirely after a few years. And, unfortunately, a few years of piano lessons in childhood will not produce the lasting capability that parents envisioned for their children.

Making a Practice Schedule Work

Summer is a good time to start lessons. You can more easily establish a practice routine during this period of relative freedom for your child.

Begin by setting aside a portion of each day specifically for practicing and help your child become accustomed to this habit.

When fall comes and the school year is under way, sit down with your child and make a daily practice schedule together (Chapter 1). Write down specific times for each day's session. Divide the practicing into sections if you like. Morning practice gets the best results, so schedule some practicing before school if at all possible. Post this schedule near the piano. If there is slippage in practicing during the year, parents and teacher can refer to this schedule or revise it as needed, to help get the child back on track.

During practice time keep the room quiet. Do not allow phone calls, friends, siblings, TV, or computer use.

If you think of and talk about practicing simply as a part of your family's daily routine like brushing teeth, doing homework, and eating breakfast, you will find that your children see it that way, too. This cuts down on a lot of needless discussion.

Parents as Practice Partners

The average child needs at least five years of piano lessons from a good teacher to build lasting skills, and eight to ten years would be a better bet. Yet most children quit piano lessons after a few years and grow into adults who "can't play a note."

How can we keep them at it?

Young piano students need help to set them on the road to effective practicing. They need help understanding directions, setting daily goals, and exercising patience when things get difficult. Above all they need to hear praise for their accomplishments. No one can do this better than a parent.

Preschool and early elementary age children definitely progress faster when parents play a part in practicing. And the rate of progress is important, because the sooner a child discovers that practicing brings results, the more motivated he will be to practice. Parental help during the first few years of study may make the difference between a passing enthusiasm and a lifelong skill.

How much a parent participates will depend on work and school schedules. Some parents are daily practice partners, sitting with the child at every practice session. Others take part several days a week or perhaps only on weekends.

What if both parents work outside the home and the child goes to an after-school program? This means that practicing comes at the end of a long day—the child is tired, and the parent may only be able to listen with one ear from a distance while performing other tasks.

But even parents who have limited time or little knowledge of music can have a pivotal influence on their children's practicing. To begin with, the simple fact that a parent shows interest and admiration is a powerful motivating factor for any child.

Some parents say, "I know nothing about music—how can I possibly help?" Actually, they might be even better helpers than parents with a musical background. One reason is that they are learning right alongside the child, not only by reading the teacher's instructions but also by asking questions of the student. This makes a child feel 10 feet tall. Second, parents who don't play themselves are often genuinely amazed at a child's accomplishments, again a huge motivator. Finally, parents may know "nothing" about music, but they certainly know how a child learns, builds discipline, sets goals, and celebrates growth.

To help their children get the most out of practicing, parents must understand what happens at the lesson and then must keep the lesson alive during the week through some form of guidance of the practice sessions.

If you do not actually sit with the student during practice time or lesson, ask the teacher to record important parts of the lesson. Listen to the recording together with your child soon after the lesson and again later in the week if questions arise. Compare the recorded lesson to the practicing you hear. Think of each piano lesson as a demonstration of how to practice. At home you should hear a daily rendition of the drills and routines that were covered in the previous lesson.

If there is no recording, read the practice assignment each week. If you don't understand what is expected, ask your child to explain it to you. If your child doesn't understand it, let the teacher know. Make sure that each item on the assignment sheet is covered.

Listening and Helping at Home

Practicing does not sound like a concert. It sounds like fragments of music being worked on, smoothed out, and put together. It's like completing a jigsaw puzzle. And as with any puzzle it is a time-consuming, detail-oriented process.

Listen to your child's practicing. You can tell the difference between good practicing and recreational playing, whether you know how to play yourself or not. Of course you want your children to play for pleasure, but with your help they will also learn to *practice* with pleasure.

Goals. Children love learning new things. They will try again and again until they succeed. But if their goals are impossibly high, they will become disappointed and frustrated. Help your child set attainable goals for each day's practicing. For example:

1. Work on a small amount of music—one section, one phrase, even one measure—at a time.

2. Focus on one problem at a time—one hand, for example, or one quality, such as accuracy, rhythm, evenness, dynamics, or fingering.

Mistakes. Children often skim over imperfections in their playing instead of taking steps to solve them promptly. A parent can give guidance on the spot by asking the child to stop and think: What exactly was the mistake? What caused it? How can it be fixed?

Praise. Most young children start piano lessons because their parents want them to. Praising day-to-day progress is probably the single most important thing you can do to keep your child playing the piano.

Praise is a powerful tonic. A 13-year-old student told me, "Sometimes kids might avoid practicing when parents are not supportive. But if parents say, 'Wow, I really enjoy your playing, you're making so much improvement,' that makes us want to do more."

Parents are sometimes ambivalent about this. A parent once told me, "It is very difficult for me to give praise because I feel that my child does not have enough discipline. I want him to pay more attention to fine details, to understand that the fine details are what make a piece beautiful." Yet this parent also noticed that "when I tell him I see improvement in his playing, he practices more happily and is more willing to work repeatedly on problematic sections."

Discipline. Students look to their parents not only for praise, but also for help in acquiring discipline.

I used to be surprised when students seemed pleased that "Parents make us practice." But then I realized that children don't want full responsibility yet. In effect, they want their parents to do the hard work of keeping away distractions and making sure the practicing gets done.

Feedback. My students count on their parents to tell them how their practicing sounds. They know this makes their practicing more effective, while at the same time they enjoy their parents' attention. A 13-year-old observed,

> "When I first started, my mom sat with me when I practiced, and we worked out problems together. She helped me to recognize mistakes and find solutions. She doesn't sit with me anymore, but I still ask her questions, and it's very helpful to know what she thinks. I would tell parents, though, don't hover over your child, because when we're practicing we want to focus, we don't want to be worried about a hovering parent."

Children like to be boss. It's better to ask them questions rather than giving them directions. How did that make you feel? What story does this music tell? What part of this piece do you like best? This approach not only keeps a child's enthusiasm alive, it's also a step on the road to analytical thinking and independent practicing.

On an off day. No one enjoys a steady job every single day of the year. Even if we like our work, we sometimes wish we didn't have to do it. Keep a list of ideas to try when your child has an off day. Some possibilities:

- Find out which practice tips your child especially enjoys doing. Stay and listen as he does them.

- Suggest a temporary change of routine—more sightreading or recreational playing, for example, or more time on a favorite piece.

- Ask that your child teach you a piece or a part of a piece.

- Ask your child to play your favorite piece for you.

- Suggest a break—maybe involving a cookie or two.

Give only positive feedback when your child is feeling discouraged, bored or fed up with practicing. There is always something to praise without being dishonest. Even if you think the playing is a complete disaster, for example, you could still say, "I really like that piece."

Practice doesn't always make perfect. Practicing is a big job for a child. It requires more self-discipline and inventive thinking than any other task. So keep in mind that, as important as it is to practice correctly, mistakes happen. Don't let your child become so afraid of making a mistake that he loses either his love for the piano or his spirit of adventure.

And remember that the habits you are helping to instill in your children are priceless attributes which will serve them well not only in music but in all areas of their lives.

CHAPTER 17
TEACHING EFFECTIVE PRACTICING

For teachers, showing students how to practice is not the most glamorous part of the job, not the most fun, and definitely not the easiest. It is crucial, nevertheless, not only because it shapes a student's playing today, but also because it sets the stage for the child's future—either for becoming an adult with a rich musical life or else, as too often happens, for becoming an adult who says, I used to play the piano, but ….

Teachers strive to make every piano lesson a lesson on effective practicing. Yet students continue to say, I don't know how to practice. Or a parent may ask, can you please show my child how to practice this piece? So apparently the subject needs constant reinforcement.

This chapter offers suggestions for that reinforcement, for helping when practicing isn't going well, and for other aspects of teaching that help a student become an effective "practicer."

Practice Tips as Tools
No teacher wants to spend every minute of every lesson describing practice drills already presented countless times. And it is difficult to write down more than a few sketchy practice suggestions while actively engaged in giving the lesson. Yet teaching students how to practice remains a critically important part of our work.

My solution was to write down practice tips, making them short, easy to understand, and useful to students of various ages and stages. This saves me lesson time and gives students a tangible tool for solving problems at home. It has led my students to more creative, thoughtful practicing and I hope it will lead to a more independent, more satisfying musical life after they finish lessons. Meanwhile, it makes lessons more enjoyable both for my students and for me.

Since I started using practice tips, my students practice better (and so do I) because the variety of tasks makes practicing more rewarding. Also, I can now devote more time to creative work in the lesson because I spend less time explaining this or that practice instruction. Instead I simply refer students to a particular drill's title. By now they know most of the tips' titles, but if they forget one they can read up on it at home. Students come to their lessons better prepared, which again saves lesson time and energy for other pursuits.

I introduce one or two practice tips at a time, not in any specific order but rather as the need arises. Once the tips have been introduced, I no longer have to go through the explanation. I can just say, for example, "Do **Back Up** on the *B* section."

At first I decide which tips each student should use and when. But as time goes on, students learn to find their own solutions. Most would rather choose a tip themselves than have me tell them what to do, which is just the way I like it. And I find that asking students to choose their own practice drills encourages them to take practicing more seriously. They also become better at recognizing, analyzing, and solving problems on their own—a skill they will need if they are to keep music in their lives after lessons are over.

Length of Lesson

In the United States, music lessons conventionally take place once a week. With once-a-week lessons, it is virtually impossible to give adequate practicing instruction to a student in 30 minutes, especially if the student is a young beginner. Children are sponges for new ideas, eager to learn, and capable of enormous progress even—or perhaps especially—in the first year of lessons. But in 30 minutes, no teacher can:

- cover technique, repertoire, sightreading, and theory

- listen and comment on all the pieces prepared during the week

- present new material

- give practicing instructions for all of the above

- have some personal interaction with the child

Many parents do not realize how much teachers need to cover in a lesson. Once they recognize the benefits of longer lessons, parents become receptive to the idea. In my experience, the most common misgiving of parents is that their child cannot concentrate for longer than 30 minutes (or 45). I am certain, however, that I can keep a child occupied and interested for an hour, so I respond, let's try it and see. No one has ever asked to go back to a shorter lesson.

Studio Practice Requirements

When I first started teaching I believed that what mattered most was practice quality, not quantity. Probably as a result, my students were good musically but weak technically. Eventually I came to understand that time counts. We may think of playing an instrument as an art, but the basis of this art looks a lot like the basis of any sport you can name—hours, weeks, months, and years of physical training.

Learning to play a musical instrument well, polishing a piece to the highest level, building a technique strong enough to serve our musical ambitions—all these things take time and discipline.

We all know that it's hard to find time to practice in this busy world.

Teachers are painfully aware that most piano students quit after a few years of lessons. Almost without exception, the dropouts are students who practice sporadically and for short amounts of time. A handful of piano students have so much natural ability that they can make progress—at least for a while—on 20 minutes of practicing a day. But normal children who skip practice days or who practice only a few minutes a day never get a chance to find out just how much they could accomplish with steady practice.

Teachers can help parents by explaining this cycle of success, or the lack of it, and by insisting on minimum practice requirements based on students' age or level of advancement. If all students and parents entered piano lessons with a clear understanding of practice requirements and an expectation of success, I believe we'd have two-thirds of our students remaining in lessons, instead of two-thirds of our students quitting.

Starting Smart

Too many piano students are taught to play notes, or to play pieces, without being given any idea how the pieces are constructed or what the music might mean. I have come to believe that teaching students to map music (Chapter 1) is one of the most important things we do, because it is a powerful tool that they can use throughout their lives to keep learning and growing in music.

Yes, mapping music does take time. Yes, some students don't want to do it. I insist on it anyway. Eventually they all come to understand how valuable it is. They realize that their knowledge gives them more facility in learning and memorizing music, stronger confidence in performance, and above all a greater understanding and appreciation of music in general.

Group Performance Classes

I find that regular, informal piano performance classes are invaluable to students. A studio recital that is the only performance of the year puts too much pressure on students. Regular performance classes give students frequent opportunities to try out new pieces, test their memory, play less than perfectly, and make friends in music. Practice performance helps students reduce performance anxiety or at least learn to manage it.

An important component of the class is learning to express ideas about music. I ask students to respond to each piece played in the class. This activity is not easy for young children. Sometimes instead of speaking they prefer to write their ideas or even draw them in pictures. So we do that, too. Students' comments often include surprisingly sophisticated suggestions for practicing. They seem to like receiving "instruction" from each other, and they take it seriously.

I notice that students practice very carefully when preparing to play in group class. Obviously, they care what their peers think of them. And of course group class is a good opportunity to play games that celebrate students' knowledge of theory, music history, practice techniques, sightreading, etc.

I hold group class for half of my students each week, so each student attends a group class twice a month. (The annual studio tuition includes a modest fee per class.) Students are expected to play something from memory every session. This could be an entire piece, two pages or just one section of a piece. The amount doesn't matter, but I make a specific assignment in advance so that students think of it as a performance and prepare accordingly. Over time the same piece will probably be played more than once. (How it changes can itself be an interesting topic of conversation.)

If you have enough students to create several group classes, divide them by age or level of advancement or both. Make your goals for the class clear to both students and parents.

I have an important hidden agenda for group classes (hidden, but not from the parents—they appreciate knowing this). Over time the students in a group class become friends. The community that they form may even be what keeps them practicing and taking lessons in lean times. To encourage this social side of things, I make it a point to take a break (with treats) and leave the room for a few minutes during each class, so they are free to talk to each other, tell jokes, relate stories from school, etc.

Although I welcome parents in lessons, they are not invited to group classes. The children feel freer without their parents. Making mistakes is less upsetting, which is important because the class includes many first-time, possibly ragged, performances.

One thing I don't allow from students in the group class is expressions of competition among themselves. The children learn not to talk about their own achievements in comparison with others and never to say anything that could hurt the feelings of a classmate. Over time they all come to regard the group class as a place where they can be comfortable as people and as pianists, a place where they strive for perfection but learn how to accept imperfection along the way. Whether they play well or not on a particular day, they know they will survive and go on to play again—probably better next time. And that's an attitude we all need to acquire.

Repertoire and Practicing

I find choosing repertoire for students both a pleasure and daunting—a pleasure because it means playing through reams of music that I love, daunting because it's difficult to find the many hours I need to do this well. Summer is my season of choice for this task.

Once I have selected several pieces that fit my view of a student's needs and my agenda, I play the pieces for the student. I ask the student to rate each piece from 1 and 10, with 10 being the best. Usually I hold out for a score of 9 or 10 to actually assign the piece. If I don't get a high rating on any of the pieces, I make another selection and try again the following week.

Since I started choosing repertoire this way, I have had no more than one or at most two cases a year of a student tiring of practicing a piece before its completion. Students are motivated to practice because they love the music.

I choose a core repertoire for each student and enter the information into a computer spreadsheet. This becomes my repertoire record for the student. It can be printed out or sent electronically to the parent, and I can see several years of repertoire information if I need to.

The core repertoire each year consists of at least one piece from each music history period, a duet and a concerto movement, plus technical exercises and etudes. I introduce this material to the student a little at a time and augment it with short pieces and sightreading books. Such a variety of tasks makes practice interesting, and completing all the tasks takes time. This is how they end up spending, and enjoying, more time than they ever thought they would practicing the piano.

What should be done if a student ceases to enjoy a particular piece? I don't mind dropping a piece that a student has struggled with too long. No pianist lives long enough to play all the great music in print, so why not spend the time we have on music we love? If I think learning a certain piece is essential for the student, I try to find out exactly what the issue is. Often the problem is easily solved if we work on it together. But if I've made all the suggestions I can and the student is still resistant, I make a proposition: you promise to practice this piece long and hard every day this week, using the practice plan I've just given you, and if you still don't like it by the time of your next lesson, I promise that we will drop it.

I rarely encounter this problem, and I believe this is because each student is involved in the choice of repertoire. Of course, when students are young I give them many pieces without consulting them. But when we select pieces that will take considerable time and effort to complete we always play the 1 to 10 game.

Technical Exercises as Aids to Practicing

Teachers often use the analogy of speech patterns when describing a musical phrase. We point out that no one reads a book aloud in a monotone with equal emphasis on every syllable, but that in fact we speak in pitch and rhythm patterns that form a kind of music and that a musical phrase also needs such variety to be meaningful.

I see another parallel between language and music. We learn language not so much one word at a time as in groups of words that we constantly hear used in the same order, with the same meaning: "Good morning," for example, or "Put on your socks" or "Hurry up." We learn, and remember, a phrase, which is then easy for us to put into a longer sentence.

I think of musical building blocks in the same way. Most teachers begin technical training with five-finger patterns and the resulting triads, broken and blocked, like this:

We do this not only to strengthen a beginning student's fingers, but also because early piano pieces, like the Bach Musette (fig. 17.1), are full of five-finger patterns and triads. A student who can play five-finger patterns automatically in all keys will learn this phrase in no time, because the patterns he practices in his technical warm-ups are the building blocks of every piece he plays.

Fig. 17.1. J.S. Bach, Musette in D Major.

Bach

Unfortunately, this close relationship of technique and music is often abandoned after the first year or two. Students are assigned a few desultory scales and arpeggios and a Hanon exercise or two. As pieces grow in complexity, students recognize fewer and fewer patterns. They can no longer produce these patterns automatically, so they must devote much more time to practicing the piece.

For years I have used a technique regimen[3] that incorporates every type of musical building block that we find in our literature: not just scales and arpeggios, but also several kinds of broken chords, blocked chords, chromatic scales, octaves, trills, and double-note scales. It starts out simply with a few skills and adds to them gradually over a period of years.

Since I have been using this system, my students analyze scores more intelligently and practice more effectively than they did when I covered only scales and arpeggios. They are better sightreaders and, most rewarding to me, they learn music faster and better because they have a whole repertoire of musical building blocks on tap. I now spend much less lesson time on correction than I once did.

Studying Music Theory
Understanding music theory also contributes to good practicing, because it helps a student navigate a musical score (Start Smart, Chapter 1).

With so many excellent theory books available, it is not necessary to offer students a separate theory class (though laudable if it can be arranged). Instead students can be asked to complete theory workbooks a chapter at a time, a level at a time, for the duration of their piano study. Many high schools offer AP Music Theory—a course my students give high praise.

On Memorizing
Earlier chapters contain a variety of tips on memorizing, something that takes up a significant amount of most pianists' practice time.

I believe in teaching students to memorize from the start, and consequently I give regular memory assignments. I like students to memorize consciously, not by chance, using practice tips to exercise all facets of their memorizing capabilities. In fact I am thinking about memorization from the moment I ask them to start smart (Chapter 1) on a new piece, because I believe that careful analysis is the beginning of memorization.

[2] Alexander Peskanov, *Russian Technical Regimen*, Willis Music.

Some children, however, are "natural" memorizers. They can memorize new music almost instantaneously, especially if they analyze it in detail. I don't see any reason to burden such students with unnecessary how-to-memorize drills, any more than I would insist that a student with great natural facility practice the same technical drills that everybody else needs. Nevertheless, I try to make sure that every child's music memory is well-rounded, that is, not narrowly based upon a single factor such as muscle memory, ear memory, or eye memory.

For most students, memorizing is a time-consuming task requiring large amounts of quality concentration. Different teachers may require more or less memory work from their students. Fortunately or unfortunately, however, pianists who play in competitive situations must play from memory. That aside, another benefit of memorizing is that a student can play for friends any time, not only at home with the book open.

Nonetheless I don't mean to suggest that every pianist must memorize. Many adult piano students, for example, play without memorizing, and that's certainly understandable considering the time and effort it requires.

I have had a few young students say, "I can't memorize". One was an eight-year-old who was conscientious in every other respect, so I took her at her word and assured her it was all right not to memorize. She used the score in group class and in studio recitals for two years. During the second year I started giving her tiny memory assignments—one measure a week for one month, the next month two measures a week and so on. After the second year she performed from memory without difficulty. She may have begun lessons with a small emotional block or maybe she had a learning problem or perhaps she was just afraid of failure. Whatever the reason, the problem disappeared in time.

Another student, a high school boy, declared memorizing to be "stupid," and said he would no longer do it. This boy played at a very high level and performed often, so once he stopped memorizing he didn't have the same performance opportunities, which seemed to be fine with him. A year later, when he visited me after one semester of college, he played an hour of memorized music for me. "What happened?," I said. "Nothing. I just felt like doing it."

Dealing with Practice Problems

It is a good idea to hear last week's problem spots first in this week's lesson. It will give you an idea of the quality of practicing your student has done. If you make a habit of this, your student will learn to expect it and will probably come to the lesson better prepared.

Earlier chapters have numerous tips for using speed intelligently, but they also ask for slow practicing. A student's idea of "slow" is usually quite different from mine. So when I want someone to practice slowly, I assign a specific metronome speed. (Parents appreciate this because most know that their children practice too fast, but don't know what to do about it. Saying "slow down" is not the answer.)

What can a teacher do when, as happens to everyone occasionally, a student has a bad week? Never let a parent cancel a lesson because a student hasn't practiced well that week. Lack of practice gives you an opportunity to do something entirely different in the lesson, to take a welcome break from the usual routine. You can present new repertoire, work on a specific technical issue, do sightreading, listen to recordings together, analyze a new piece, listen to the student practicing, and so on. It can be enjoyable and productive for both teacher and student.

What can a teacher do when a bad week turns into a bad month? I generally consult the parent first. I ask how the student is doing at school, at home, in other outside activities. If there is an issue larger than piano practice, I need to know that before talking to the student. If the problem seems to be only in piano, I ask how the practice schedule (Chapter 1) is working. That often leads to a long discussion and a solution.

Sometimes, however, a parent is just as puzzled as I am about a lapse in good practice habits, so then I consult the student. Some questions I might ask are:

- How is your practice schedule working?

- Are you happy with your progress?

- How is school? What's your favorite subject? Who is your closest friend? (There might be issues at school that shed light on the practice problem.)

- Do you like the pieces you're working on?

- What do you like about practicing?

- What don't you like about practicing?

- Do any of your friends play instruments? Do you ever play for or with each other?

- What piano piece would you love to play some day?

- How many hours of sleep do you get on school nights?

CHAPTER 18
STUDENT, TEACHER, PARENT INTERACTION

Parents of piano students are eager to help their children advance. They often ask, how do I know if my child is practicing correctly? This is a profound question, one that teachers should be asked and one that teachers need to address repeatedly with both students and parents.

The teacher may say, first of all, that playing a piece over and over again is not practicing. But, then what is practicing? This is hard to answer. A person could practice effectively in a hundred different ways. Good practicing never stays the same. It changes from hour to hour, from day to day, from year to year. That's because our moods change, our capacity changes, the music itself changes, and our perspective on the music changes.

All this is just as true of children as it is of seasoned professionals. So, in training students to become good "practicers," a teacher should be able to offer enough effective practicing tools to serve a variety of students' needs. And parents should make themselves aware of these tools and encourage their children to be creative in using them.

IN THE LESSON

Chapter 16 discusses the value of parents sitting in on lessons. This is the most obvious example of the practice triangle in action. If a teacher endorses this practice, following a few guidelines will help keep it effective.

The primary goal is the student's concentration, and every student/parent interaction is unique. Sometimes the parent can sit very close, sometimes sitting across the room works better. If the student is ultrasensitive to the parent's presence and has trouble focusing on the teacher, it's best for the parent to sit outside the student's sightline.

The parent can be an avid observer at the lesson but should leave the talking to the teacher, again to avoid breaking the student's concentration.

If a parent has questions, the best practice is to raise those questions during the lesson, but not at the last moment while the next student is waiting. It's good for the teacher and parent to have a general plan for when questions should be brought up. And the teacher can help by pausing at an opportune moment and inviting questions from the parent.

At Home

Where and when do students learn to practice? The model is the lesson itself, which is in essence a practice session with the teacher as guide and partner.

But does the student follow up in daily practicing? Not necessarily. This is where a parent's help is invaluable. By attending the lesson or listening to a recording of the lesson, a parent knows that a variety of practicing techniques were laid out. The task then is to oversee the child's application of those techniques at home. This does not necessarily require musical expertise. It is more about systems and structure than it is about music.

However, neither parents nor students can be expected to fully absorb every idea presented in a lesson, no matter how dedicated they may be. They need concrete tools to work with at home. For example, the parent should make sure the student has a metronome and knows how to use it. A practice log may help. A recording of the lesson keeps the material in mind. There should be a weekly assignment sheet and a variety of practice tips to choose from. These are all tools that a teacher provides or suggests in order to help the parent help the student.

Teachers need to make practice requirements clear to student and parent alike, and parents must see that the requirements are carried out (Chapter 16).

On the Same Page

Parents and teacher should check every once in a while to make sure they are sending a consistent message to the child. Sometimes a parent needs an explanation of a teacher's system or philosophy or goals. Teachers should regard this situation as an opportunity, not a challenge, realizing that the better a parent understands the process, the more the student benefits.

As Time Passes

As a child grows older, the practice triangle changes. Everyone still has a role, but there is less interaction. As a student's expertise deepens, there may be less frequent or no parental attendance at lessons and little direct supervision at home. Instead, the parent's role becomes more one of general support and positive feedback.

Meanwhile the student/teacher bond deepens. With this new relationship often comes a greater sense of responsibility on the part of the student, which gradually replaces the earlier model of a parent being in charge of practicing.

Now the parent and teacher may see less of one another. They still need each other, though, especially in times of difficulty. A teenager may be going through agony in some non-musical facet of life, and the teacher needs to know that, even if only in a general way. Similarly if a student starts to waver in enthusiasm or work or attitude in the piano studio, it's time for the teacher to call the parent.

Each adult in the practice triangle is, at different times, a parent, a teacher, a coach, a refuge, a disciplinarian, an inspiration. The student passes from childhood through adolescence to the cusp of adulthood, experiencing subtle changes in his relationship with teacher and parent. The final formal act of the practice triangle might be a gala senior recital to celebrate having shared so many years of hard work and joy in music.

CLASSIFIED INDEX OF PRACTICE TIPS

This index categorizes the practice tips by the subjects they address.

ALPHABETICAL INDEX OF PRACTICE TIPS

GENERAL INDEX